ESCAPE
FROM TERROR

ESCAPE FROM TERROR

PAUL MURDOCH

CROSSWAY BOOKS · LEICESTER

CROSSWAY BOOKS
38 De Montfort Street, Leicester LE1 7GP, England

© 1996 Paul Murdoch

English language edition published by arrangement with the Finnish
Evangelical Lutheran Mission.

First published 1996

British Library Cataloguing in Publication Data
A catalogue record for this book is available from the British Library.

ISBN 1–85684–151–0

Set in Bembo
Typeset in Great Britain by Parker Typesetting Service, Leicester
Printed in Great Britain by Cox & Wyman Ltd, Reading, Berkshire

CONTENTS

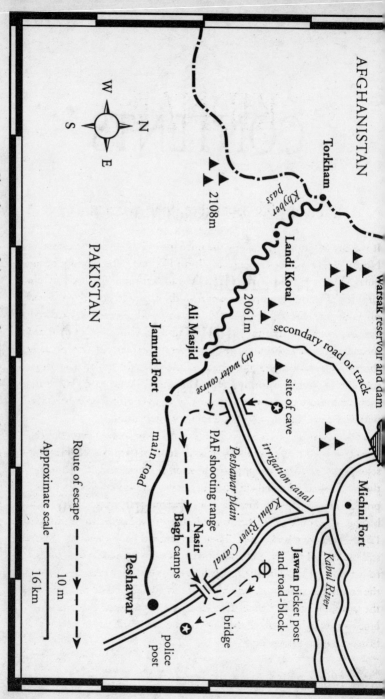

Sketch map of the area of NW Pakistan described in this book

KIDNAP

Sunday 9th September 1990, 8.05 a.m.

It was my favourite drive along the outskirts of Peshawar, the capital of North West Frontier Province in North Pakistan. The serenity of the quiet road that follows the irrigation canal around the back of the airport was so much more pleasant than the crowded Arbab road lined on both sides for kilometres with car parts, furniture and hardware bazaars, with its traffic jams, dust and pollution. Canal Road meandered lazily through rustic scenery. Besides, it was actually shorter this way along the edge of the triangle which the three subcities of Peshawar formed from University Town to the Cantonment, the more modern part of the city of over a million inhabitants with its Saddar Bazaar, GPO and military installations.

It was Sunday. Ever since Zulfikar Ali Bhutto had changed the working week to accommodate Islamic lobbies, Sundays had become schooldays. I had just dropped my boys off at school and, since I was in the area, had stopped in at our new colleagues' place before proceeding to church for the consecration ceremony of the new bishop. It had been their first night in their new home, and I thought I'd see how they had coped. They had seemed happy enough, Marja still in her night gown and Haikki with no shirt on yet. It was too hot to get dressed up. The sky had still not lost its dusty grey tinge since the end of the monsoons which meant there would be no real break in the weather for some time. Everyone was waiting for that first clear blue sky which signalled the end of the inversion layer keeping a blanket on the baking earth.

Escape from terror

Why didn't more people use this short-cut from University Town to the Cantonment? The tarmac here on this raised canal bank was in poorer condition than the main road, I thought, as I slowed for the 'speed-breaker', or 'sleeping policeman', a ridge of clay piled up across the road to force the traffic to come to a slow roll. This one was a private affair; the owner of a small mosque on the other side of the canal was collecting contributions towards refurbishing his place of worship. I wondered whether people would be more inclined to donate to the grizzled little man sitting on his string bed at the roadside, astraddle the speed-breaker, for having made them slow to a crawl. It certainly didn't awaken higher feelings of generosity in me. But was it generosity that inspired Pakistanis to give to such causes? They viewed these solicitors and even beggars as an opportunity to earn *sawab*, merit, with Allah. The beggars behaved as if they were doing you a favour by demanding that you give to them 'for Allah's sake'.

As the last of the *pukka* brick houses and tin-fronted shops of University Town dropped behind, almost emerald-green fields of maize opened up to the left of the road, interspersed with the yellow-green stubble of mown fodder patches. Clusters of houses were visible here and there in the distance. The other side of the canal was the dusty grey the sky got its colour from. It lay higher and was without irrigation, tribal territory – outside the jurisdiction of the local government and its police forces. It didn't occur to me that that was perhaps why few people used this road.

Through the tinted windows and with the air conditioner on, everything appeared so rich in hue, inviting. In an hour or so the sun would be so glaringly bright that all colours would fade and flatten out. Not even the air conditioning would be able to belie the heat of day in its merciless intensity. But for now the illusion of an inviting countryside, tranquil and idyllic, held.

The fields ran into the mud walls of a village on my left and I caught a glimpse of the volleyball court that made the place seem so likeable to me. It was proof that there was life in the village, people socializing and having fun together. The boys and younger men gathered there in the evening after sundown and *maghrib* prayers, bringing the otherwise deserted-looking place to life. During the day, with the women inside and the men at work in town, the only signs of life were the occasional boy running before a cloud of dust, pushing the rim of a bicycle tyre with a stick, or a young girl shooing her goats to greenery they were allowed to eat.

As I looked back at the road I realized that I was being overtaken. An older car that had once been metallic green before the years of merciless Pakistani sun and sand had ground and faded it to a nondescript blighted lime, was forcing me over.

My attention was drawn away from the vehicle itself as angry-looking men protruded from the overtaking car, hanging out of the windows just a few feet from me, brandishing AK-47 'kalashnikov' assault rifles and automatic pistols. There were more guns than men poking out of the windows, but even so, two had managed to squeeze heads and shoulders together out of the rear window. Their car slowed to my speed instead of overtaking. Why were they threatening me? It wasn't just a show of Pakistani male machismo like on election days. Had a child been hit by a car back in the last bazaar and did they think I'd done it?

My mind churned as my stomach turned. I would have to clarify the mistake, stop the car and talk it over. That was the way things were done. One had to take the offensive, keep talking. After all, I knew I hadn't hit anyone, unlike the time a man had jumped out in front of my car from behind a lorry and come crashing through the windscreen. Even then, the instantaneous crowd that assembled hadn't been violent with me or my elder son, whom I had had to pick up in shock from the midst of the glass from the exploded windscreen, even though they were Pathans, who are not known for their forbearance.

The men would scream and throw a tantrum, that was the accepted behaviour. I would have to choose the most influential, take him in a friendly way by the arm, walk him around to the front of the car and dramatically wipe my hand along the bumper before holding it up to him to determine whether there was any blood on it. Perhaps I would run his hand over it for good measure. Contact was important here.

People weren't afraid of touching or being touched. Grabbing hold of my beard and swearing I was innocent would clinch it. Grabbing hold of his beard would be a last resort. Better not to, if it could be avoided, because that might be understood as begging for mercy and therefore admitting guilt. On the other hand, done with a slight shake of the head and a roll of the eye, it might get one out of a tight spot.

Most important, I couldn't wait to see what would happen, I had to be on the offensive, never for a moment allowing any slack. I had to stay in control. Had to keep my face, not let on that I was intimidated by their guns. Showing fear too, would be tantamount to admitting guilt. I knew it wasn't going to be easy, but there was no alternative. Accelerating and trying to make a break for it would convey the same message. They might start shooting then.

The thoughts were buzzing by so fast, I couldn't stop to ponder. These were gut reactions, responses to the programming of four years of intensive study and living with Pakistanis. By the time I had stopped the car we were well out of the village and their car passed to block me. Before I could get out and approach, a bearded, turbaned, cursing Pathan jumped out of the front seat, his long, loose and unkempt *shilwar-kameez* dress billowing as he charged my car and bashed in the window on the passenger side with the butt of his kalashnikov. Sticking the muzzle of his AK-47 through the shattered window he drowned out my protest with curses and commands to get out of the car. While he was covering me on the left, two others untangled themselves from the window of the door, which a fourth in his zeal had opened before they had drawn themselves back into the car, jumped out and joined the attack on my side of the car. Their clothing, like that of the first to charge, identified them as rural Pathans, but from the Pakistani side of the border. The narrowing cut of the leg of their loose shilwars showed they were not Afghans. Usually warring Afghani factions caused the trouble here in University Town: bombings, kidnappings and political assassinations. I quickly rolled down the window to remonstrate with them and to avoid having it, too, knocked in my face. I abandoned all thoughts of sauntering up to the man in charge and decided to stay in the driver's seat. So much for staying in control! The only control left for me was damage control. I did turn off the ignition switch though – out of habit. The mission's ten-year-old station wagon with the recently fitted air conditioner stalled anyway as soon as the engine went into idle, and accelerating the engine to avoid stalling would just make it boil; it always did.

Anyway, I wasn't even remotely thinking of trying to drive away from this situation. These tribal Pathans were really mad! It would take some effort to calm them down, I thought, simultaneously trying to get them to tell me what they wanted while they tried dragging me from the driver's seat with brute force. One had opened the door a little and was hitting me with his rifle. Another was tearing at my clerical collar through the open window, ripping my shirt open as if he thought he could pull me out through the window, inadvertently keeping the other from getting the door fully open. The third was butt-beating me on the shoulder and head with his automatic pistol. He was scared. It was written all over him. I guessed this was taking too long for him. He seemed in an awful hurry to settle up. He pulled back the slide on his pistol, loading a round into the chamber to get his point across. They wanted me out of the car. Now!

The bearded fanatic who had led the attack ran around to my side of the car as I rose from the driver's seat. I had begun to fear that they might exact 'justice' right there without clarifying first that it was really me who had run over the child – or whatever it was that had happened to get them so furious. I addressed the bearded man, who was obviously in command, in Urdu, sometimes called Hindustani, the *lingua franca* of Pakistan and Northern India, where the form used by Hindus is called Hindi. My frenzied attempts to get them to tell me what this was all about only made them more angry and brought more blows and more Pushto curses. I let them push me in the back seat of my car. My heart sank as I caught a glimpse of my briefcase with the church's 25,000 (£600) rupees in it and the oriental carpet intended as the church's going-away present for the interim bishop folded up next to it in the back of the car. When they found those valuables they would be bound to get even more greedy in their demands for 'compensation'. They would take all this as a 'down payment'. A bird in the hand . . . they wouldn't even care whether I had really done whatever had happened.

The three others crammed themselves into the back seat with me and my daughter Anna's baby seat, as the front seat was covered with glass splinters. The doors wouldn't close. But the car wasn't starting in spite of the bearded man's concentrated efforts.

'What did you do to the car?' he demanded in Urdu, turning a furious face to me to force an answer.

'Nothing!' I replied truthfully. I hadn't pulled the anti-theft switch under the driver's seat, which cut off electricity to the coil. My eyes were riveted on the two black knobs at the bottom of the dashboard, which somehow grew in size to fill my whole field of vision. It had to be the air conditioning. It was turned on and the battery was probably too weak to turn the engine over with it engaged! Despite his frantic attempts, he couldn't get the engine to start.

'What did you do to the car?', he demanded again, if possible even more furiously than before.

'Nothing!' I replied again while he shouted orders to the others. Why were they in such a desperate hurry? Was it just their adrenalin, I wondered? Two of the assailants got out and tried to push start the car. There was no response from the engine. The fifth in the gang, who had kept their car running for the minute or two in which this had all transpired, backed up and rammed us from behind, but still the car wouldn't start. I began to feel a little calmer. God hadn't deserted me. Their plan, whatever it was, wasn't working!

In the gang's panic I was dragged from the car once again and shoved between two of the thugs in the back of their dilapidated car and from there onto the floor. I was told in Pushto and pointed 'body language' to stay down on the floor and not to look up. A woman's veil was thrown over my head and the muzzle of a pistol pinned it in place.

The truth hit home with a deadening finality, with the realization that I had missed my chance to escape. These people were gangsters or some sort of fanatics after all and this wasn't just an unfortunate misunderstanding. There had been no accident, there was no point in talking sense and proving my innocence. As the car started it struck me: no-one had driven past. Were there no eye-witnesses? Would there be no-one to report my kidnapping? How would anyone be able to know what had happened to me? Would the next passer-by steal the car, the money and the carpet, leaving no trace?

The car sped along the poor road, then jerked violently to the right. Had we just crossed the canal into tribal territory? Or had we already reached the junction of Canal and Airport Roads? We covered uneven ground – turned and turned again. We lurched and careened. My head was between my feet against the floorboards. How would I overcome the nausea? My body began to awaken from the initial shock to the pain. I couldn't move my right arm. There wasn't any room to anyway, but there was no response in the muscles or nerves there. Was it just the agony of being cramped up like this, or had I been injured when they had beaten me? I couldn't tell with no room to move. It wouldn't be wise to move anyway with two guns on me, one on my head, the other in my ribs.

In the midst of my fear, pain and confusion, words started repeating themselves in my mind, blocking out everything else. 'The Lord is my shepherd, I shall not want, the Lord is my shepherd, my shepherd, my shepherd, he leadeth me beside the still waters, my shepherd, my shepherd . . .' A strange sense of calm began to spread over me. But was I deceiving myself? Thinking how just the repetition of a *mantra* may bring comfort and peace of mind to a Hindu, even though its true meaning is not understood, I began to doubt. Was it just the rhythm of the words, the vacuous sense created by the magic of the syllables, the subconscious childhood reminiscences associated with the twenty-third Psalm that soothed and comforted me in my total vulnerability? I didn't want to fool myself, I wanted to face the facts.

I tried to stop the flow of the ancient poetry. It wasn't just the rhythm, wasn't just the repetition, it wasn't an unreal 'mantra-effect' that was buoying me up, sustaining me. It was the message: The Lord is *my* shepherd. Even when the words stopped, the calmness remained. I needed to hear that very much right now. It was comforting for me to realize in my desperation that God truly was looking after me. Even now, in this hopeless situation he was caring for me and even leading me. Hadn't he saved the car, the valuables? Wouldn't he save me?

The car lurched more and bottomed out bringing me down against the driveshaft well. They had left the roads and were taking me to or through the tribal area outside the jurisdiction of the police, avoiding the police checkpoints along the way which were intended to stop this sort of thing from happening, I reasoned. With the calmness that Psalm 23 was spreading in my heart and mind as it repeated itself to me over and over my mind began to work more clearly: my friend and colleague Heikki and his wife Marja, whom I had visited just a few minutes earlier, would be coming along that very stretch of road any minute now. I had recommended this 'short-cut' to the church to them. To think that I had felt we had chosen a safe place for them to live! Heikki just had to put his shirt and tie on to be ready for the big function we were all going to: our Peshawar Diocese in the Church of Pakistan was consecrating its new bishop at 9 o'clock this morning. If no-one else beat them to the car, Heikki and Marja would see it standing in the middle of the road, keys in the ignition, doors open and window smashed in. They would realize what had happened and inform everyone. The money, the carpet, the car would all be rescued from otherwise certain theft. I breathed a sigh of relief: my family and the police would find out right away.

My family . . . How would Marja-Liisa take the news? Tuomas and Henrik, the poor boys, would they be able to continue with school? To think I had just dropped them off a quarter of an hour ago, when would I be able to hug them again? And little Anna? Consciously she would suffer the least, being only 21 months. But the situation was bound to take its toll on her subconsciously. And then our unborn baby – would Marja-Liisa be able to carry it to full term? 'Oh God Protect Marja-Liisa and the baby!' I whispered under my breath. As the prayer ended the psalm returned: 'The Lord is my shepherd, I shall not want, he maketh me to lie down in green pastures, he leadeth me beside the still waters, he restoreth my soul!'

In an odd, paradoxical twist of my emotions, I felt somehow

relieved. Was it the psalm? There was something more, too. Suddenly it hit me: it was a relief not to have to be active at the consecration and ensuing festivities. I had worked so hard in the past months to help pave the way for it and to 'keep the boat afloat' until we could resolve all the problems standing in the way of electing a new bishop. I had done my job. Stood between the competing candidates and parties, trying to mediate and always being suspected of being partial to one or other of the candidates. After all the threats and slander that had been a part of my job, I was just glad it was over. Now it was time for the others to celebrate. All the difficulties and intrigues involved had taken the joy out of it for me. Still, I felt a responsibility and a concern for the whole situation. 'Lord, make the day a success, but even more, enable our new bishop to guide the church towards a more fruitful life and witness in this community. Let the church be a witness to your love and mercy,' I breathed in silent prayer.

We were back on a decent road again, I realized, as the bumping and rattling stopped and we sped along an even, paved stretch, the ringleader in the front seat urging the driver on. It didn't last very long. Again a sharp turn and unpaved road. I tried moving my arm, this time there was response, but the pain was excruciating. My left leg had gone numb, but again, it was the same problem: there was no room to change my cramped position. I wiggled my toes furiously trying to bring the circulation back. We bounced across what must have been open country or along a dry river bed. Again a paved road and then what seemed to be a gravel track. The men were quiet, I could sense their tension. They spread a blanket over their laps, covering me at their feet completely. The car slowed down – was there a road block? Would it be police, army or some local chieftain? The bandit on my right was muttering some threats under his breath and pressing his pistol in my ribs. The car kicked mildly as we traversed the speed-breaker without stopping then picked up speed again. The men broke out in disdainful laughter. We must have passed a checkpoint without having to stop for inspection.

Had we been driving for half an hour, forty-five minutes? From my cramped condition it had been too long in any case. The man on my right reached over and felt my pulse. Was he afraid I had died on them since I hadn't been moving? They hadn't beaten me that badly. Did he want to ascertain whether I was calm and relaxed, or my pulse racing with fear? He held on to my wrist until we were apparently clear of civilization. I was told to sit up and the chadar around my head was fixed and tied as a blindfold. My glasses were in the way; I took them off, but the man to my left snatched at them and I felt them bending as he wrenched them from me. They were steel framed. I hoped I would be able to bend them back into shape if they gave them back. My nausea ebbed with the upright position. I was able to breathe freely at last. But my right arm seared with pain at the touch of my neighbour.

'Are you American?' the man in the front asked in poor English.

'No, I'm Canadian.'

'What your country?'

'I'm from Canada.'

'British? Angrez?'

I gave up and nodded, *Angrez* doesn't mean only English, but foreigner in general, if of European background.

'Who you work for?' He continued the interrogation.

'I work for the Church of Pakistan.'

'What is Church? You pay from Gornament?'

I explained to him in Urdu that 'church' means the place where Christians worship. Being a Pathan, his native tongue was Pushto, but we were able to communicate on a primitive level in the lingua franca.

'How much money you have?'

'About two thousand.'

'Give me!'

It took some time for me to get my wallet out of my hip pocket with my sore arm, wedged in as I was between my two guards. There were some satisfied grumblings from the front seat. He turned and yanked the Afghani silver and carnelian ring off my ring finger. People had sometimes asked in an approving way whether I was Muslim when they saw that ring. They believed carnelian had a special religious significance (somewhat like the jewels in the walls and gates described in the Book of Revelation). Some felt it had healing qualities, others protecting ones. Some kissed the stone after prayers, touching it to their forehead, lips and heart. The man on my right was interested in my watch and took it. The ringleader tugged at the gold cross and chain around my neck until the chain broke. My mother-in-law had given it to me as a birthday present a few years earlier.

'What else do you have on you? Are you carrying a gun?' I let them frisk me and check all my pockets; they even remembered to check my waistband in the small of my back.

As I laid my head back and let them get on with their search I noticed that I could see out of the slit at the bottom of the blindfold. Judging by the shadows in the car we were travelling north. No, we had turned east, then south – endlessly changing direction. We came out at a metalled road and turned west, skirting some foothills. Everything was dry and barren. The clay and rock soil still had a warm colour in the morning light. It couldn't have been more than nine-thirty, maybe even less, but we had been driving forever . . . The road wound lazily in a generally northern direction. On the left, between the road and the foothills a small water channel or runoff drain showed that we must be near civilization now, because wherever water was to be found in Pakistan, people were abundant.

The bearded man in the front passenger seat glanced back and noticed that he had missed my wedding band when he took the ring off my other hand. I didn't mind them taking the other things and the money so much, but the initial satisfaction I had felt at them missing my wedding ring turned into deep disappointment as he forced it off my finger. I wondered, with a tinge of suspicion, so totally foreign to me otherwise, whether their taking the cross and wedding ring meant anything. Would I have no more need for them?

Had we left the road or did it peter out? We were in a dry river bed where Pathan villagers were digging gravel and loading it onto one of their colourfully decorated trucks. The village stood on the far bank. As we passed the truck I was pushed down into a lying position and covered once again with a man's chadar-blanket so as not to be seen. The way up the river bank was blocked so we turned right.

Once back on the road we continued on for some time until we reached a cluster of mud houses. There was electricity because a power pole stood in front of the largest of the buildings, a typical Pathan *kor*, a mud house and courtyard surrounded by a twenty-foot-high mud wall and guarded from a watchtower with slits for firing from on the corner nearest the full-height gate. We slowed enough for the ringleader and the bandit to my left to jump out of the car, leaving only two in the front seat and the two of us in the back. It was almost luxurious to be able to have half the back seat to myself and change my position so that blood could flow in my limbs once again. I wondered why it was not at all painful to lie on my bad arm, whereas trying to move it was excruciating.

The church service would be well under way now, even if it had started late according to local dictates. What would people think of me not turning up? Had Heikki found the car and informed Marja-Liisa and the bishop? It hurt me to think of my family not knowing what had happened to me. I hoped the church money and carpet for the bishop hadn't been taken or the car itself – it was worth 150,000 rupees (£4,500: a year's salary for me). No, not even the most primitive would think that I had taken off with the church's money! But would anyone really understand what had happened? Would they have the presence of mind to ask someone else to step in for me where I had a part in the service, robing the new bishop? Pakistanis were past masters at improvisation, there would be no trouble even if they noticed I was missing only when my turn came in the service. How fortunate that Bishop Malik had kept the ring to be presented to the new bishop last night when he had asked to 'see' it and not given it back to me, pocketing it instead! Fortunate also that the clerical gowns I had had sewn for some of the participants I had left in the sacristy. As ordinary pastors they couldn't afford to buy their own. Providence was at work.

How hot it was under the chadar and difficult to breathe! I tried to keep my mouth free so as to get some fresh air. My guard pulled it back down over my mouth, I shoved it back up again. He pulled it down. I protested that I couldn't breathe. My persistence paid off. They didn't want a suffocated hostage: I was allowed to lift the blanket high enough to breathe as long as my face didn't become visible. This

Kidnap

year's long, hot summer hadn't yet relented and the temperatures were hovering in the upper thirties centigrade. By lifting the blanket, through the slit at the bottom of my blindfold I could look up and out through the window. Electric and telephone lines and trees lined the road now which was obviously paved as the surface was smooth. We must be in Barra or Ddara in the tribal area, I thought.

We stopped at a large house with lots of dogs barking. We had to wait for some time. Standing as it was in the sun, the heat in the car was unbearable. The driver backed into the shade and everyone but me got out to stretch and rest. With the whole seat to myself I was able to roll over on my back and make myself reasonably comfortable for the first time in an hour and a half. Then the car began to fill up again. I had to curl up to one-third the width of the small car's back seat; the man on my left just sat on my hip and wiggled his way down until he had compressed me into the space available.

The young man who got into the front passenger seat seemed to be in command. He hadn't taken part in the kidnapping, but took over from here. Had he put these desperados up to it in the first place? He was well dressed and spoke in a refined voice in contrast to the men who had accosted me. I knew that voice! Who was it? My friend Abid's brother, Syeed, the carpet merchant! I strained to get a better look through the slit and chadar, but didn't dare to lift the latter. He was cleanshaven except for a neat moustache, like Syeed, but it just couldn't be him. They lived in Dabghari, behind the mission hospital between the Old City and the Cantonment. I had been to their home on a couple of occasions, the last for Abid's wedding. Syeed would be opening up the shop at the Dean's Hotel, just now, if it was getting on for 10 a.m., wanting to catch the tourists as they left their hotel rooms on their way to the bazaars. He was always the first one there unless he was on a buying trip. His father, the only sports angler I knew in Pakistan, and his other brothers came to the shop later in the day.

'Is it a woman or man?' he asked.

'*Mard* (a man)' came the reply from the one on my right.

'Foreigner? What nationality?'

He weighed the responses according to his own business instincts. He never asked to see me, but being a man, who never covered his face with a chadar, he did not realize that I could see him sitting in the front by looking through the gap between the front seats. Not the details of his face, but his clean, cream-white shilwar-kameez dress, his neat moustaches and clean-shaven chin. He directed us to a place where he asked the guard at the gate for Mohammad Gul. The guard replied that he was out and not available. After a short wait we drove on to the outskirts of the town. The cultivated gangster had the car stop and asked a young boy where to find Hakeem Gul. Why didn't the man know his way around? Wasn't he from this town? Had he just come to meet the car? Was it possibly Syeed after all? Would that be good or bad for me?

The boy got in and we drove a short way. He gave further directions before getting out. We went on a few hundred metres where the cultivated young man left us to wait in the shade of a tree. The engine stalled and the man to my right, who seemed to have taken over command from the bearded fellow who had led the attack on my car and jumped out at one of the villages along the way, cursed the driver and told him to keep the motor running. From then on, if we ever stopped, the car was backed up and pointed in the right direction for a quick getaway, should it be necessary. The well-dressed, well-spoken young man returned and consulted with my captors: 'It's not going to work, take him out in the desert fifteen miles and finish it!' Or did he mean 'finish him'? The sentence was ambiguous. My heart sank. Were they going to finish me off? Would Marja-Liisa be left alone with the kids? Again my mind was filled with the words of the twenty-third psalm: 'Yea though I walk through the valley of the shadow of death, I shall fear no evil, for thou art with me, thy rod and thy staff, they comfort me . . .'

As the confusion from the initial shock subsided, I wondered whether I had misunderstood. Were they intending to 'finish it' by letting me go in some deserted place, where I wouldn't be able to tell from where they had brought me? Perhaps that was it, they would make me lie face down at the side of the road with my eyes blindfolded and fire a few warning shots over me as they sped away, so I wouldn't be tempted to look after them and get the car number.

Kidnap

No, the way he had said it, he meant to finish me off. They would make me kneel by the side of the road with my eyes blindfolded and the muzzle of a gun at the back of my head . . . I waited for the click before the explosion, but couldn't think the thought, couldn't see my execution, my body collapse as it would have to. I couldn't think the thought of death. Not really, not practically. All I could see was the final frame of a picture depicting life, my life, its last moment. With my thoughts now collected, I realized there could only have been one meaning to his words. I had only wanted them to be ambiguous. He had preceded his directive with some questions: Had I seen them when they abducted me? Would I be able to identify them? It seemed to me that the men, speaking in Pushto, of which I only understood a little, had answered in the affirmative, *kha*. Perhaps, he, too, had wanted there to be a way for them to free me, but I could give incriminating evidence. In any case, his orders had been precise and business-like.

Did it all end here? Could it be that my time had come to meet my creator and saviour? Didn't I have anything more to contribute to God's work? Could it be that my whole life led only to this bleak point in the badlands of the North West Frontier Province? Hadn't I had anything to give? Had it been a waste? I couldn't fathom it. But did I have to understand it? Why was I always trying to understand everything? Did it matter whether I understood it or not? There was the fact. This was it whether I understood it or not. I wanted to understand. Or maybe I just wanted there to be meaning, meaning in my being. Wasn't that what life was all about? I needed to let go of what I could no longer hold on to, let go before it was torn away, find dignity in release. God knew why. He was the one who had to know why. That had to be enough. God's grace had to be enough. Was this the same answer St Paul had received to his desperate pleas for release from his own troubles? 'My grace is sufficient for thee.' It wasn't the kind of answer that is easy to take. But it was the only answer I got.

At the same time a kind of stubbornness arose. I wouldn't beg for mercy, no matter how much I clung to life and felt despair at the prospect of imminent death. I wouldn't grovel. I'd tell that man giving the advice that he should pull the trigger himself. The sin would be on him. It was so easy to get others to do your dirty work for you! The thoughts whirled in my mind leaving an empty dizziness and a sense of confusion, frustration and shame. Was I just trying to prove to myself that he couldn't beat me? Was my condemnation of his cowardice a judgment greater than death? Whatever it was, I let go and was surprised to realize that coming to grips with the fact that my life had been spent began to take the edge off my fear of dying. I found release in faith, I found I could let go. A moment came when I felt ready for death. But it was only a moment. Such readiness can, by definition, be only momentary, an instant of lucidity cutting through the haze which surrounds our human limitations in everyday life, an instant that one is tempted to regard as a delusion only a moment later.

Had the car started off towards the desert, or were we still standing in the shade of the tree? Everything but the question of death was crowded out of my consciousness. My life did not roll off like a film before my eyes in an instant. The past was not my concern, the future was.

There had been other times when I had been face to face with death for just a moment. I would guess that most people had been prior to the final encounter. Once in the early eighties while spearfishing for the Bible School I was teaching at in the South Seas I had dived after a green turtle only to find that it was being chased by a huge deepwater shark and that I had come between the predator and its prey. I had never felt such terror as I did while watching the shark approach. Even though the shark had swum past without taking any notice of me, its sensors locked on to the turtle, and even though I had made it onto the reef, I had trembled as I stood there. I had had to force myself back into the water. Then there was the traffic here in Pakistan. We as a whole family had barely escaped death on the Grand Trunk Road that leads the way across northern Pakistan and India joining the Khyber Pass and the port of Calcutta when a huge, yellow National Logistics Cell rig had careened into our path only to get control at the last instant, but forcing us off the road. Fortunately, the embankment had been wide and without obstacles. Then, too, we had trembled and barely dared to get back into the traffic, we were so shaken. But I'd never experienced what someone with a terminal illness must face, or the prolonged possibility of being killed in war.

This experience differed greatly from those fleeting moments of terror I had faced before. The possibility of imminent death hung over my head like the sword of Damocles, hanging from only a hair. The fear would be with me for more than just an instant, it would be for fifteen whole miles, if it had been meant as an actual measure and not a substitute for 'far enough away from civilization for no-one to hear the shot'. What would the effect of the wait be? Would the same terror grip me at the last moment, when death was inevitable, or would the lucidity and preparedness return to sustain me? Was I only calm now because I secretly hoped and maybe even believed that he had meant they were to let me go? I didn't know my own thoughts. Whichever way it went, fifteen miles was an awful long way to go. My thoughts were prayers: 'Lord, if it is your will, help me to be able to face it . . .' Again the words of Psalm 23 filled my consciousness and brought solace: 'The Lord is my shepherd, he leadeth me, he leadeth me . . .'

CAPTIVITY

Sunday, about 10.30 a.m.

I didn't have to weigh the question of life and death for the time it takes to drive fifteen miles along Pakistani desert tracks. Just five or ten kilometres after dropping the mastermind off in the town we arrived at a place that reminded me in its vague outlines perceptible to me through the coarse chadar of where, earlier, the two members of the gang had jumped out on the way into the town. The road had the same feel to it. The distance was right, we had driven only a quarter of an hour or so and the high-walled *kor* was situated just as the one I had seen vaguely through my blindfold. Everything was in reverse as we were now coming from the opposite direction. During the last hour or so my blindfold had become so loose that it was not hard to see up and out through the window. With the blanket covering me most of the time, no-one could tell whether the blindfold was in place or not.

Obviously the men weren't following the instructions. They had caught me, why should they listen to the *dalaal*, the broker crooks used to fence their 'wares'. He hadn't been able to handle the job. They would decide among themselves what to do with me, carry the job out without anyone's assistance.

What had they decided to do with me?

The car pulled off the road and climbed an embankment until it stopped. My blindfold was opened without removing it from my head. It was rearranged to fall over my head and shoulders like the woman's veil it was. The men wanted it to look as if a woman in *purdah* was being helped out of the car, should anyone be looking.

Captivity

Again it helped that these men had never worn a veil and didn't realize that I could see out, although they could not see in. While we had been travelling, it had been wrapped like a turban, only a little lower, so as to cover my eyes. I had gone to every effort to make sure they could not tell I could see out as they would think that I had neither recognized any of them nor the route we had taken. Now, too, I put my hands out in front of me like a blind man, feigning to be afraid of stumbling or bumping into something. The actual dwelling with its enclosure loomed high in front of the parked car, its double steel doors, large enough to let a lorry pass through into the yard, closing out the world and its intruding instincts. What went on behind those walls was the business only of the head of the extended family living there. His word was law. We weren't going that way. The three men stood around the car door, shielding me from prying eyes, helped me out of the car and guided me a few steps off to the side where there was a lower mud-walled building. While two of the men stood to either side of me, the third lifted a bench to the side and unlocked the padlock to the chain on the upper corner of the door. It opened into a single room with no other exits. I was led in and sat on a *charpai*, a string bed, which someone disengaged from a pile of the ubiquitous wooden pole frame cots with rope or reed netting as a mattress.

They signalled me to sit on the cot. Someone retied my blindfold, doing a better job of it. One of the men poured luke-warm water into an aluminium bowl and held it to my lips to drink. It was the first drop of moisture all morning. Normally, I would have declined it, taking care not to cause offence. People here were sensitive about their water and quick to be offended if their guest thought he was being offered impure water. But I didn't have a choice. I needed the fluids. Someone else told me to take off my shoes and lie down. One of the men took me by the wrist and guided my hand to where the *lota*, a spouted water pot, was to be found under the bed when I needed another drink. This must be the place they were going to keep me, since they had taken the trouble to bring me a supply of water.

As I lay on the bed I tried to take stock of the situation, recounting what had happened. I tried to imagine what my family must be going through and what my colleagues would be undertaking, all the while listening to ascertain whether anyone else was in the room with me. Something was being dragged in front of the door, probably a charpai for the guard, even though it sounded more like a big stone. They had locked the door from the outside when they left, hanging the chain attached to the upper left-hand corner of the door itself onto the hook of the door-lintel and padlocking it, reversing the procedure I had witnessed outside when we arrived. Were they going to post a guard in case I tried to force the door, or were they jamming the door for the same reason? Could it be that they had barricaded the door because they all were leaving? As if to confirm my thoughts, the car started up and backed down the hill, sending a shower of gravel as it left.

It was deathly still both inside and outside the room. They must have run off and taken cover somewhere. Yes, the car had driven off, but then again, it was very unlikely that no-one would be left behind as a guard. And if he were left alone, he wouldn't make any noise . . . There was no-one in the room, I was sure of that. I had been here perhaps ten minutes already and there had been no movement, no sound of breathing, no cough, nothing. I removed my blindfold and looked around the room. It was a *hujra*, a gathering place for men outside the restricted area of a family's private home, where women's faces might be accidentally seen, bringing shame on the household. It was a mud structure some four by five metres. In the middle of the room there was a raised mud platform with a large reed mat on it where the men would sit to share a meal or take tea. Several charpais stood on the mat. The roof was supported by four wooden pillars at each corner of the platform. The builder had sawn a criss-crossed design into the posts. My charpai stood along the side wall to the left of the door. Yes, it definitely was a common-room for the men of the vicinity. They had not taken me inside the kor as I had first assumed they would. If I were to try to escape, I would only have the door and the guard to get past, no high mud walls, no gate . . .

It was dark inside, hot and dark. There was an electric panel on the wall with wires leading in, but no bulb in the socket. That would tally with the power pole I had seen when passing here on the way into the town an hour or two ago. The only ambient light filtered into the gloomy room through two small ventilators high up in the wall on the other side of the platform. The ventilators must have been facing north since the sun cast no shadow and was itself not visible through the openings. The colour of the sky was already the dusty light greyish blue of a hot summer midday. It would be at least another month before the sky would clear to a true blue.

I wondered about my chances of escape. Would I be able to fit through one of those holes in the wall? They had no window panes. Perhaps if I went head-first and on my side then I could pull myself through to whatever was outside. They looked just big enough, or were they a shade too small? It would be no problem to climb up on a charpai leaned against the wall . . . But first I would have to look at the surroundings: how many houses were there? What was the lie of the land like? Would it offer any shelter if I were to make a break for it? That was it! I needed to relieve myself, urinate. They could hardly refuse to give me five or ten minutes privacy. I would fix the blindfold so I could see out. If there was a gully or ravine like the one we had crossed just before the village, I would run for it and keep to the near bank, so that no-one could take aim at me. We still had to be somewhere in the Peshawar valley, we hadn't climbed enough to leave it. My guess was Darra Adam Khel, the infamous illicit drug and weapons centre of Afridi territory. We had driven much longer than one needs to reach Barra, even considering the circuitous route we had obviously driven. I could envision the washed out *wadi* or dry river-bed I would follow out of the Darra valley into the Peshawar plateau until it passed under the road leading to Peshawar some fifteen kilometres out of town. If I could only catch them by surprise and beat them to the river-bed I felt confident that I would be all right. I would outrun them even though I wasn't in very good shape as I hadn't been able to jog this last year due to an ankle injury. I would run for my life! Once I reached the road I would wait at one of the many speed-breakers built across the road. In true Pakistani fashion I would jump onto the back of a bus when it slowed for the speed-breaker (so it wouldn't break something else) and jump off again before we reached the station. I didn't have any money to pay the fare.

Maybe I wouldn't try that trick after all . . . I could flag down a car and ask for a ride. That way I wouldn't have to deal with any angry conductors. Anyone could see that I was a foreigner even if many Pathans are fair and being caucasians have the same features as Europeans. I couldn't remember ever seeing a Pathan in western dress, though many Punjabi businessmen, teachers and officials wore it to work. Someone would be sure to give me a lift. Once in the greater Peshawar area I could hail a three-wheeled Vespa riksha or a horse-drawn tonga and pay when I got home.

There was a noise outside before I had time to get up and look through the ventilator. I quickly fastened my blindfold in preparation for whoever was coming. The heavy object was dragged away from the door, the door-chain rattled and some men entered the room. But they hadn't come for me, they were carrying the upended charpais out of the hujra. Perhaps there was enough shade for them to sit next to the wall outside. No, one of them was moving towards my string bed. He sat on the cot at my feet and started to interrogate:

'What's your name?' he asked in passable Urdu. It must have been the man who had been sitting on my right in the back seat who had 'taken charge' of me after the attack on my car. It was his voice and he had heard me speak Urdu to the man in the front seat when they had taken everything on me but my clothes.

'Paul Murdoch.'

'What country are you from?' It was the same questions all over again. They must know by now who I am, they had had lots of time to go through my wallet. There was a photostatic copy of my passport and my driver's licence showed my address. My heart sank again: they would know where Marja-Liisa and the children were, that is unless the Finnish Evangelical Lutheran Mission, which had sent us to Pakistan, recalled them to Finland when the truth about my kidnapping became evident. I hoped they wouldn't send anybody to the house. No they wouldn't, that would be too dangerous, they might run into the police. What were the police doing? Had they borrowed one of our mission vehicles as they had when one of our cars had been stolen, so that they would be more mobile in carrying out their investigations? The thoughts flashed like lightning through my mind as I fielded his questions. It was no use trying to mislead him, but I would need to be careful about what information I divulged. 'Wise like a serpent, but without guile like a dove . . .'

'Why wouldn't the car start?'

'How should I know?' I felt like telling him that God had preserved the car, but thought better of it.

'It was because the air conditioning was on, wasn't it?'

'The battery is a little weak,' I answered truthfully, avoiding confirming his doubt. Was this fellow a bit brighter then the bearded man to reach the solution himself?

'Who is going to make your arrangements?' he demanded.

'No-one will pay a ransom for me, if that's what you mean,' I said, not so convinced as I said it — it would depend a lot on the circumstances. Would the Finnish Mission be able to withstand the pressure? It was a two-edged sword: they had to secure my release, but they wouldn't want to establish any precedent that would make other Finnish missionaries lucrative bait and objects for future kidnappings. I had no idea whether the Canadian government had a policy on the matter.

'Do you have a brother?'

'He died more than ten years ago.'

'What about your father?'

'He's not here, he's in Canada.'

'Where do you work?'

'I work for the Church of Pakistan.'

'What is "church"?'

'It is where Christians worship.'

'You are not a Muslim?'

'No, I told you I am a Christian.'

'You mean Isai?'

'Yes, I am a follower of Jesus.'

'Do you believe in Muhammad?'

'Muhammad is your Prophet, I serve Jesus Christ.'

'Do you believe in the Koran?'

'There are four books. As a Christian I must follow the first three: Torah, Psalms and the Gospel. Those are the books God gave to us Christians in the Holy Bible. Your Prophet agreed with this.'

'So you are really Isai?'

'Yes.'

'Good!'

'Why is that good?'

'Because we will get a lot money for you!'

'You won't get a lot of money from anyone. The Christians in this country are mostly very poor, living in abject poverty. And if anyone does give you money for me it will be God's money, that is, if you want to do this kind of business with him!'

'No, we won't take it from them. We'll get it from the government.'

'The government won't pay anything for me, I'm a foreigner.'

'They will have to: the Isai will go on strike through the country from Peshawar to Karachi. There will be no-one to empty the night soil and in two days the whole country will stink to high heavens. There will be so many complaints from high-powered people that the government will be willing to pay any price we set!'

This degrading and caricature-like view of Pakistani Christians all being sweepers disgusted me. Of course many Christians were sweepers, perhaps even the majority in our part of the country, where this degrading and stigmatizing work was the only job they could get. Very few Muslims were willing to sweep and empty the night soil in the buckets employed as receptacles in the older houses where there was no sewerage. Still, the derogatory attitude and the willingness to take advantage of an oppressed minority made me sick.

'The Christian sweeping community will not go on strike. They haven't yet and won't now for my sake either,' I countered, hoping to discourage him and wishing to get away before anyone ended up paying any money for me.

'They will go on strike, the Christians always stick together!'

Captivity

'I don't know, I'm not too sure . . . ' I tried to weaken his resolve and discourage the idea, secretly being grateful that at least this aspect of the loyalty within the Christian community was known to him.

'I know and you'll see. You've got nothing to worry about,' he replied. The matter seemed settled for him. It definitely was a relief to know that they were going to keep me for ransom and not finish me off as the young mastermind had seemed to suggest. Let him hang on to the hope, then, that the government would give them hundreds of thousands, maybe millions, if it meant safety for me!

'Will you phone and let my people know I'm all right? My wife and children will be worried about me.'

'Its against our principles. We never make contact ourselves. That is the duty of your people.'

His use of the word 'principles' (*asuul*) grated against my nerves. It wasn't even ironic, it was heresy.

'How should my wife and kids know how to get in touch with you?' I asked, knowing that my Muslim friend Tariq or one of the Church leaders would already be sending out feelers to try to locate me or the people to deal with for my release, employing maybe a *dalaal* of their own. Yet I wanted my family to know that I was alive and well as soon as possible. Ever since another European had gone missing and was suspected dead some months back, one had to reckon with the worst happening and I did not want my family to have to face that mental anguish.

He wrote my telephone number on his hand, the poor man's diary.

'What was the cheque for 100,000 rupees (approximately £2,300) that you had in your wallet?'

Again my heart sank. I had fooled myself into thinking that they might not understand what it was. It was a bank draft from bank to bank in my name to transfer mission funds from Tank to Peshawar accounts. It was not crossed and was a bearer draft, so if they could get me to sign it twice on the back, anyone could pick up the money at the cash counter. Did they know that? Would they force me to endorse it? Could I use it to barter with them for my release? Was that why I hadn't put it in the safe; would it secure my release? For a moment the temptation was great to try to make a deal. On the other hand, they already had the cheque and might try to force me. Besides, it was wrong to use the mission's money for my personal gain.

Most missionaries had a thing about mission funds. They were God's money, holy funds. If they tried to coerce me should I sign wrongly so they wouldn't pass the cheque at the bank? Should I write 'deposit to' . . . and then sign? Should I cross the cheque if they gave it to me to sign? Should I cancel it, tear it up? It was an awful lot of money in these parts, which dedicated people had donated or raised for the work of the mission. They would probably keep me until they had the cash in hand anyway, so any tricks would just bring revenge down on me. There was no time to think things out in detail, no time to make plans, the man was waiting for my answer.

'It was for the work of my organization.' There was no reaction. Had he lost interest, or had he just wanted to make sure it was a cheque and not an invoice or some other piece of paper unknown to business in the Frontier, where huge sums changed hands with a mere handshake or a man's word? Honour was written with a capital 'H' in these parts. Tribals guarded their own honour and punished a lack of it in others. If dealings went outside the tribal infrastructure, terms were strictly cash. No-one accepted cheques. That was why armed guards stood at the doors of every bank: many customers came or left with plastic bags, attaché cases or even suitcases full of cash. Would they dare to risk identification by going to the bank? There were the armed guards standing shotgun at the door of the bank to think of. And the cheque could only be cashed at the branch it was issued for, on the main 'Saddar' road, smack in the middle of the Cantonment business district. It wouldn't be easy to get back to tribal territory from there if things went foul.

My colleague, Maija-Leena Pajari, had given me the draft the day before and suggested I put it in the safe, but I had wanted to get it to the bank right away. Sunday in Pakistan is a banking day – or half-day, as one frustrated bank official had once told me, because it is useless for them to stay open all day when they can't raise any financial institution anywhere else in the world on the telex. I had taken the cheque with me in the hope of getting away from the celebrations before closing time at 1 p.m.

Maija-Leena would be sure to remember the draft and check the safe in our home: I hoped she would alert the bank. She had the draft number on the receipt I had given her the night before. If she only had the presence of mind to think of it in the confusion that would ensue over my disappearance. She had to get to the bank quickly. 'Lord, help her to remember!' I breathed to myself.

Someone else entered the room with tea.

'Do you want your tea hot or cold?' the man asked, meaning did I want to let it cool before drinking it. I couldn't wait.

'Hot is fine, thank you.' My interrogator took my hand and placed a small, shallow Chinese tea cup with no handles common to this area on the tips of my fingers as I held my hand out cupped upward ready for it. It was hot and too full. As I was blindfolded, I spilt the hot liquid into my hand. He took the cup back, spilt a little onto the dirt floor, then returned it. The tea was black, hot and sweet. I drank it greedily. The intensity of the suspense and uncertainty had sapped me of my energy.

'All the people are poor here, we can't afford to put milk in our tea,' he said, explaining why there was no milk in the tea. It was as if he were embarrassed at not being able to offer proper hospitality to a guest. Buffalo milk was an absolute must for tea offered to guests. I didn't care about the milk, and in spite of his almost-apology, didn't feel like a guest. I needed the sugar and drank cup after cup until the small pot was empty.

'You know, we weren't after you, you just happened to fall into our hands. We had been trying for someone else, the son of one of the local big-shots who drinks the blood of us poor people. They are so corrupt, they make life unbearable for us. But Allah didn't want it, the kid escaped our grasp. His Pajero jeep had armed guards. We spent the night in the desert and returned to town this morning looking for another catch. Allah sent you along to us, it was his will!' Had they really blown the job the day before and come back? It didn't seem likely. On the other hand, the boys' branch of the Beacon House

School for the elite was on the road near to where they had picked me up. Had they been on their way there when they saw me? Perhaps they had been late. School would have started at eight, ten minutes earlier. They could have easily missed the child's car and continued to prowl until they spotted me.

'Who made the plans,' I asked, 'you or God?'

'That doesn't matter, we are Muslims and always do God's will, no matter what it is we do. You know, it's not such a simple thing to roam about the cities with kalashnikovs for which we have no permits! We have been recognized, this is *janbazi*, a game of life and death! We can descend on a city only once, maybe twice a year at the most. We have to get illicit weapons, a getaway car, it all takes money and our children are starving.'

'Why don't you get a job, do some honest work for regular pay?'

'There is no work.'

'You could drive a truck.' That was the most common livelihood for these tribal people with no economic base other than transport, be it legal or traffic in illicit goods. Many drew their livelihood from smuggling, which they seemed to view as a more honourable form of handling freight.

'There are no f—ing trucks.'

I wasn't going to be able to convince him taking this line.

'Highway robbery, kidnapping and extortion are never God's will – don't put the blame for this bad piece of work on him! And what do I have to do with it all? What have I done that gives you the right to detain me?'

'You must have done some sin or another, this is God's work! He is punishing you for it.'

'Yes, I am a sinner. Everyone is in need of God's mercy and grace. Yet I do not believe that God has put me here to punish me. I am his servant. I have come to Pakistan to serve him. He will take care of me, whatever his purpose in allowing this! You should let me go.'

'Tell me why the car wouldn't start,' he began all over, 'it was because the a/c was on, wasn't it?'

'It was God's will so.' It was time to turn the tables.

Captivity

'It was the a/c,' he said half to himself, not willing to accept that God might not have wanted him to have that car.

He got up from the charpai and made for the door, telling me to get some rest. As he was closing the door, my plan came back to me – after all I did need to relieve myself.

'I have to make water,' I called out to him in the local jargon.

I fished for my shoes with my feet as he came back to my string bed and grasped me by the hand, leading me just a few steps towards the door. Instead of taking me out, he turned me towards the corner.

'Here?!' I asked, incredulous.

'Yes, right there!'

'You mean right here in the room?'

'It doesn't matter!' came the reply. He was waiting.

'It's all right, I'll find my way back to the charpai,' I said, wishing him gone. My plan hadn't worked I realized; I hadn't even made it out of the room, let alone rearranged my blindfold so I could get a view of the lie of the land. So much for that plan, it must not be time to try an escape yet, I thought. My interrogator hadn't left. I could sense his presence at my left shoulder. It was disgusting.

'You're not hungry, are you?' he asked in a tone of voice that seemed to imply there was no food anyway, even if I were. Again it was the cultural mandate relating to hospitality that made him ask, I thought.

'Not particularly.' I really didn't feel like eating, although it was past noon and I had only had a little yoghurt at seven that morning, delicious, tangy Pakistani yoghurt. He led me back to the string bed and told me again to get some rest.

As I lay there, the thoughts came rushing back. Had the consecration ceremony gone smoothly? It seemed so far away and insignificant in the light of my situation. How is it that people get worked up over whether the general supplications are before or after the laying on of hands? And then the reception after the service was over. Were there any problems feeding the guests? We had counted on 1,500 and had made preparations for a few hundred more. If only no-one had to be turned away. That would cause big problems in the Christian community, where hospitality is written with just as big a capital 'H' as among the Muslims.

Escape from terror

It seemed as if an eternity had passed since eight o'clock that morning. How was the family taking it? Word must have reached them by now that the car had been found with a window smashed in and the keys in the ignition – or had it been stolen by some passer-by? Would the church's money, the chequebooks, receipts, the bishop's carpet ever be recovered? Would anyone think of picking the boys up from school within the next hour? What would they go through when they heard? Would they be able to grasp it? It was at times like this, when I thought of my family and their ordeal, that a lump formed in my throat. Was it a defence mechanism that my alter ego kept telling me this was not real, it wasn't really happening, it was all illusion? Finally my fatigue overpowered me and I drifted off to sleep.

Sunday, early afternoon

The distant rattling of the door chain brought me in stages out of a deep and exhausted sleep, which had cut me totally off from the necessity of facing the reality of my situation. Before I was fully awake and aware of what was going on the gang was getting me up and leading me out of the door. There must have been no-one in sight as they made no effort to make it look as if they were helping a woman into the car this time. Again I was made to lie down, cramped in between two guards on the back seat of the small Japanese car. They covered me with a large men's chadar, the all-purpose sheet or blanket carried by tribal Pathans when moving about. I was reluctant to let myself be crowded into that same excruciating position so stretched my feet to the door and under the front seat, forcing the man on my left to shift his feet, and pushed my head up onto the left knee of the man to my right. Neither objected in the slightest and I was reminded of the realization I had made once while travelling on Karachi buses: Pakistanis don't mind physical contact with complete strangers. It is normal, one of the facts any traveller has to live with. From then on, I shifted and squirmed about whenever an arm or leg went numb. I was surprised to find that my right arm didn't hurt with me lying on it. But it was hard to breathe under the chadar. Besides, with it on top of my blindfold, I couldn't see anything. I tried lifting the sheet and holding it against the back of the front seat to give some breathing space. It helped a little, but my hand was pushed back down. I protested that I wasn't getting any air and folded the chadar back off me. I was drenched with sweat. My guard on the right replaced it. I pushed it back. This kept up until he gave up and let me keep it off my face at least, except when we were moving through populated territory. I agreed knowing that it was the only way to get some wind from the open windows when we were clear.

We had been travelling for some time, changing directions every few kilometres, sometimes even sooner. Where were they taking me? There still must be road blocks they were avoiding. I had the feeling we were following the general direction of the Peshawar–Bannu road, which passes through Darra Adam Khel, but taking side roads except where it was necessary to travel on the paved road itself. The men were not talking much among themselves. The cassette recorder had been going the whole time and they only had two tapes they switched between. One was typically monotonous Pushto singing, the same woman both sides, and I, at least, couldn't tell whether the whole tape was one song or a collection of similar ones. The repetition and monotony had a hypnotic effect over the hours. The other was an Urdu film sound track. Both were bad quality recordings, but the men seemed to enjoy it, sometimes raising their arms in dance motions and switching the tape each time it had played through. I had a headache!

Judging from the colour of the sky it must have been late afternoon, around five-thirty, six o'clock. In two and a half hours one can cover a lot of ground in a car, even on bad roads. We must be well beyond Kohat now, somewhere on our way to North Waziristan, the wild no-man's land hopelessly far away from the law, what existed of it in this country, and impossibly out of reach of civilization. It would be next to impossible for me to escape.

The discussion I had had with the one who spoke Urdu had convinced me that they were intending to hold me for ransom and there was no danger to my life at this point, as long as they did not know that I had seen their faces! Were they banking on that in keeping me against the instructions they had received this morning? But if they were taking me this far it might take time to negotiate my release. My secret hopes of a quick release began to fade.

The car slowed to a stop. We must have been at a tribal road block. The tribal *maliks* or chieftains controlled their own areas in this way. My guards warned me, *khatarnak illaqa* – danger area!, covered me up and were leaning over me. There was some discussion going on between the people at the road block and our driver, but the car wasn't searched and we were allowed to proceed. I pulled the chadar back off my head and could see through the window that it was dusk. But something was wrong. We were driving into the dusk, going east. All the time I had thought our general direction was south and west. We had been on the road for some four hours now. Maybe we were about to arrive at the final destination and the only approach was from the west . . . Somehow it didn't make sense, we were on a major road and still backtracking. Then we pulled off onto a dirt road and headed north. That fitted the picture better if they were taking me into Waziristan. We passed through a small village where dogs chased our car and came upon another road block, but were allowed to pass without stopping.

Darkness gathered and the car stopped. The others got out and I enjoyed throwing the chadar off and stretching out. There was talk of water and a 'hotel', that is, a simple wayside awning with charpais where tea and a meal can be had. I heard the men gulping down water. Soon they offered some to me in a wide aluminium dish, the kind country folk used because it was multi-purpose, used among other things as a lid to cover the opening of the wide-mouthed clay water jar. Who knew how safe it was to drink, but I could hardly ask them to boil it, and besides, I had already drunk plain water in the hujra. I would just have to trust that my stomach would stick with me and I wouldn't contract any of the more serious diseases like typhoid, cholera or hepatitis. I needed the body fluids after sweating all afternoon under that sheet. The Urdu speaker helped me out of the car. My clothes were soaking wet and the breeze felt wonderfully cool as it blew through the open doors of the car. I was all cramped up and it was not easy to move.

Captivity

'You all right?' he asked.

'My limbs are stiff. The circulation has stopped from being so cramped-up.'

'What do you think it was like for us?!' he countered, indignation in his voice. 'We've been sitting in the same position all afternoon! One's blood can't flow!' Somehow his appeal failed to rouse any feelings of sympathy in me.

'Is it dark already?' I asked, gathering that it must have been, since I couldn't see anything at all from beneath the blindfold any more.

'Yes, you want to walk for a bit?'

'Yeah, I need that!' He led me a few steps along the dirt road; something was approaching and he froze in his tracks, grasping me by the arm.

'It's a bicycle, be still.' The cyclist rolled past showing no sign that he had noticed us.

After I had relieved myself, we made our way back to the car. Since it was dark I was allowed to sit up. No-one seeing the car pass by would recognize that I was blindfolded. We soon left the road and seemed to be crossing open terrain. The car was bottoming out continuously. Where did they put the petrol pipe on these cars, I wondered, imagining the conflagration that we would be engulfed in if it ruptured and caught fire. They couldn't be planning on using this car any more, the way they were driving it; as the man had told me, they had got this car just for this one job. They needed to succeed, if only to cover their costs.

We were in uneven territory, climbing. For some reason or other, the man on my left called out, '*Waziristan zindabad* – long live Waziristan!' and undid my blindfold, using it to cover his own head from the back and the side so that I would not be able to identify him later. But there was no doubt about it, it was the man who had been sitting on my right before the car had stopped a short while back. They had changed places. The man in front next to the driver and the man on the right now also hung cloths over their heads to avoid recognition. Why had they taken my blindfold off in the first place? Was there something they wanted me to see?

Escape from terror

We were in a wash, a dry river-bed, following a track perhaps some jeep had made. We dived and lurched along the uneven *wadi*. I couldn't tell where the track went and neither could the driver at times, as he sometimes stopped, reversed and turned off in another direction. He wasn't the man who had driven when I was kidnapped. He hadn't even been a party to the abduction. So this was the man they had drummed up while I had slept in the hujra.

In the darkness it looked as if we were entering mountainous terrain. Especially to the right of the wash there seemed to be an abrupt ascent.

The car stalled and wouldn't start again. Were we out of petrol? We'd been driving for long enough. Perhaps this was to be my chance?! Would they have to leave the car and walk? They wouldn't dare to march me off under cover for fear of being seen with a foreigner, even though it was night and seemed far off from everywhere. They would either let me go to fend for myself or finish me off if they thought I could compromise them. I couldn't see any other realistic alternatives just then.

The driver was a young fellow, maybe twenty. I guessed that he was driving because he knew the way to the hideout they were going to keep me in. At least no-one was giving him directions as to which track to follow.

All the men piled out to push-start the car, except the bearded man next to the driver, who told the kid to get out and push. He himself slipped over behind the wheel. He must have been the man who had driven at the attack on my car. He also seemed to be in charge here. The car started at the second push – someone muttered, 'the motor is too hot'. I hoped it would seize up, but we continued on and there was no more engine trouble. We climbed the embankment of the river-bed and passed a small mud house where a teenage boy stood in the doorway, clearly visible in the headlights. It looked as if he was wondering where the car had come from at this time of the night. The houses here seemed to be built along the edge of an aquaduct. The gang ignored the boy and dropped back down into the river-bed. There was plenty of water around and we had to traverse puddles and streams. At a particularly large puddle we had to circumvent I was impressed by an elevated aquaduct that spanned the fifty yards of river-bed at a height which the car could just manage to pass under. The houses had been built along its course. We couldn't be too far from civilization with this much water available, I reasoned. The big puddle was caused by a spill where water was gushing out under high pressure from a leak.

We turned right under the aquaduct and began to climb the river-bed we had been following. The headlights showed the terrain rising steeply on both sides now. We were moving up into the mountains. Waziristan was a mountainous place, I thought, remembering the rugged terrain from my trips to Bannu and Dera Ismail Khan on church and mission business. With every kilometre we drove, my situation got worse.

Lights showed up in the rear-view mirror. The driver instinctively accelerated. All four men turned around to judge the situation: whether we were being followed or this was coincidence. I saw their faces in the light of the car coming up from behind as they turned, but the young man who was showing the way motioned for me to be blindfolded again. Were we getting close to the place they were going to keep me? Did he want to keep me from being able to recognize any landmarks that might help me to escape? Or was he concerned that I had had an unrestricted view of their faces? Why had they undone my blindfold in the first place when they had called out 'Waziristan zindabad'?

Those few minutes of sight would prove later to be invaluable. They avoided talking as much as possible, but over the last few miles there had been repeated talk of getting a *daksun*, the colloquial for a Japanese pickup used as all-purpose transport cum taxi in areas with bad roads needing high ground clearance. (The 'ts' sound is difficult for Pakistani speakers, they meant a 'Datsun', a Nissan, or some other make of pickup used as taxi, bus and all-round transport vehicle in rural NWFP.)

We had lost the car – it had probably just been local traffic. The track got worse and worse, the going was slow. We drove on for about an hour in silence. My thoughts became prayers again as they had so often that day.

The boys must be going to bed now, help them to be able to get some sleep, take away the fear that must be plaguing them, give them peace of mind . . . Help Marja-Liisa to cope. Who will take the boys to school in the morning? Will they go at all? You know what is best for them, help them through all this uncertainty and trouble. Anna has no idea what is going on, but she is bound to sense the insecurity around her. Be especially close to her, help her to remain the happy little twenty-one month old darling she is. Don't let Marja-Liisa's difficulties be compounded by having to deal with cross and upset children!

Along with these thoughts the twenty-third psalm, or more precisely snatches of it, kept coming back:

'I shall not want . . . I shall not want . . . I shall not want . . . I shall not want . . . He leadeth me beside the still waters, still waters . . . still waters . . . He restoreth my soul . . .'

It was even more beautiful to me in the Urdu translation, which most accurately renders the original Hebrew text: 'he restores my life . . .'

The car was climbing a steep gradient, then suddenly plunging again, only to rejoin its ascent. Could this be a road? The car pulled up, stopped and reversed, tracing the shape of the new moon of Islam into the gravel and sand as it did so. Everyone got out and my blindfold was removed. The horizon to the west showed only slightly more light than the rest of the sky – the sun must have set at least an hour ago – but the mountains were silhouetted by the faint glow. Otherwise it was totally dark. No lights on the mountainside, no vehicles moving about the valley. Was this a totally deserted area?

A man carrying an AK-47, with its long, curved ammunition clip and hollow steel-frame butt, approached from above. He had been waiting for us. How in the world had they got word to him at the distance we had travelled. There could be no telephones here! It was so dark I couldn't recognize any faces, only shapes against the ultramarine sky. We were standing on a broad path that was obviously used by vehicles – there were slight impressions in the dry shale and rock track from the wheels of cars or jeeps that had passed through here. Yet it wasn't a proper road. The Urdu speaker took me aside while the others huddled together for a conference.

'You will be well taken care of here, you'll have everything you need: bread, water, a charpai, bedding, cigarettes, tea. Go for walks, enjoy a holiday – you're in Murree! You won't lack anything!' He lifted his hand with thumb and forefinger pressed together and extended to illustrate that not even my slightest need would be overlooked. Was he trying to be humorous? Or was he sincere? Did he think that his saying I shouldn't take this personally would really make a difference? Still, there was something in his behaviour that bespoke a sort of common courtesy. He was not mean or even angry. To him it was obviously nothing personal, just business.

There was a cool wind on the ridge where we stood and it did indeed look like Murree in the darkness, except there were no lights on the hillside. But to the south in the distance there were city lights, just like Rawalpindi's lights when looking down from the 'Galis' in the Murree Hills. It seemed about the same distance too, maybe 25 kilometres as the crow flies. It had to be either Bannu or Kohat. My guess was Bannu, after all, we had driven an hour and a half in the morning and some five hours this afternoon and evening! Yes, it had to be the mountains just north of Bannu in North Waziristan. If I could only get to the road, I'd manage somehow to get on a bus or 'flying coach' heading back to Peshawar. It would only be a four hour trip, I'd get the money for the fare somehow, even if I had to beg for it. That's it, I realized: I would go to the mission hospital or to the pastor's house in Bannu and ask them to loan me the money.

At that time I didn't know that Dr. Pennel, the founder of the mission hospital and mission school in Bannu had also been kidnapped by Pathans several decades earlier, but after gaining the respect of his captors had been released.

'We will come every day at this time to check on you and let you know how the negotiations are going. Don't worry about anything!' He went over to the man who had been expecting us and I heard him say '400 rupees . . .' Had he just paid for my room and board, or was he promising the man 400 rupees (£10) to 'take care of me'? For a day? For a week? For how long?

Four hundred rupees is nothing, but then maybe these people in such remote areas were so poor they were desperate for any cash they could lay their hands on. It struck me as true to form that the man who had complained about how the big-wigs 'drank the poor people's blood' was hoping to get millions out of my kidnapping, yet only offering a pittance to this poor man.

My captors piled into the car and drove off back down the valley. I was left alone with my new guard. He started off up the ridge, motioning for me to follow. Another snatch of the psalm accompanied me: 'Yea though I walk through the valley of the shadow of death, I shall fear no evil, for thou art with me . . .'

'Fear no evil'!

Sunday, 9 p.m.

As we reached the crest of the ridge my new guard stopped and froze in his steps. He was looking ahead, where I could make out the outline of a house perched on the ridge. There was no watchtower, just the shape of a long, relatively low wall straddling the width of the ridge. It was the kind of place where medieval feudal lords would have built their castle: easy to defend, approachable only from one side. He was studying the foreground of the house. Yes, now I could see, there was movement, someone was walking across the open space between us and the house. But we had not been noticed. The shape disappeared down the hill to our left and we continued forward. My guard rattled the door chain and the door was opened after a short wait. Instead of entering, he waited until the scuffling of retreating feet had subsided before opening the door for me. Was it a woman who had opened the door, a woman he did not want me to see, or didn't he want that person, whoever it was, to see me?

We crossed the inner courtyard which was some ten by ten metres

Captivity

and sat down on charpais placed on the veranda facing the door through which we had just entered. The veranda was built up off the ground so we could both see out over the enclosing walls and catch the evening breeze too. The gentle wind was invigorating after the heat and closeness of the car. The walls enclosing the house and courtyard were made of slate and stone piled up without mortar to about three metres high. A lone, newly planted peach tree stood in the middle of the yard, which showed no other sign of life.

My guard got up and walked behind me to an earthen jug in the middle of the veranda, he poured some water into a wide aluminium dish and drank, then offered some to me. It was only the third time that day that I had had water to drink and so I drank deeply, although the water tasted muddy. They must draw their water from a shallow well, I thought. I hoped I wouldn't contract hepatitis, but decided I would just have to stop thinking about that danger, there being no alternative to eating and drinking whatever they offered me.

'You not hungry, by any chance?' he asked in broken Urdu.

'How should I not be hungry when I've not eaten anything all day!'

'You mean they not to give you any food?'

'They didn't feed me at all.'

He rose from his charpai and made a noise at the door leading off the side of the veranda to another section of the house until it was opened. He issued orders, the door was locked again from the inside and he returned to his seat. That must be the women's side of the house – had he given some instructions for preparing food for me? We sat some time in silence. The stars were magnificent. I couldn't remember ever having seen such a sky full of stars.

I felt vulnerable to the enchantment of the starlit courtyard and its confinement which seemed somehow unimportant in view of the limitlessness of the firmament. Was I so susceptible to the moment because of my utter confinement all day, being blindfolded and held in cramped conditions for over twelve hours? It was exhilarating to sit on the string bed and be able to look into infinity. 'In the stars his handiwork I see, on the winds he speaks with majesty, though he ruleth over land and sea, what is that to me?' What was it to me? The words of the well-known song from my childhood struck me as a challenge. What was it to me, the assurance of God's unlimited resources even in my confinement? I felt it as a challenge. My faith was being put to the test. This was where I would find out if God could be counted on in other than normal situations.

So this was where they were going to keep me. God is 'out there', the stark beauty and the grandeur were inescapable. But I also felt very keenly that he was close by as well, giving me peace of mind, in control of the situation that I could not control. A strange sense of peace and well-being settled over me, there was no need to fear for anything, my life, my family, my health . . . 'Thy rod and thy staff, they comfort me . . . yea, though I walk through the valley of the shadow of death, I shall fear no evil, for thou art with me, thy rod and thy staff, they comfort me . . .'

The door behind us opened and my guard fetched the food that had been made for me. The bread was delicious after fasting all day. It was different from the *naan* or *chapatti* flat bread made elsewhere in Pakistan, Afghanistan and India. The wheat was much darker and the bread much thicker, more like a cake of bread. With it was a small tin bowl filled with hot fat that smelled of fried egg, but had no taste to it. Anyway, it was a good source of energy! It was dark, otherwise I would have noticed right away that a deep-fried egg was floating in it. When most of the fat had been eaten up by dipping the bread into it, I came across the egg. Amazing how satisfying simple, coarse food without even salt could be! But there was salt, it had settled at the bottom of the bowl. I didn't know that oil didn't absorb salt. The salt was the best. After sweating all day with little to drink I craved it. There was some black tea left over from some earlier meal. It was cold, but welcome. There was no water to wash my greasy right hand, the 'clean' one that one ate with in this society, so I rubbed my hands together until the oil was fully absorbed as I have sometimes observed Pakistanis do, particularly women, whose hands would otherwise dry out from the harsh lye soaps, washing soda and rough detergents they use.

'What is "bread" in Pushto?' I tried to get a conversation going in Urdu.

Captivity

'Urdu na poiem' he replied in Pushto. I waited. 'Urdu don't know.' he translated himself into Urdu.

'Bread?' I persisted, lifting the bread basket.

'Tikala' – 'mare.'

'Egg?'

'Uwaija.'

It wasn't much of a discussion, but it was better than the total silence of no communication at all.

'Baithho – Sit!' he directed me, although I was already sitting, and laid down himself. I guessed it was time to sleep.

Sleep came easily after the stress I'd been through, but I soon woke again. The wind was bothering my sinuses. Besides, I needed to use the toilet. I sat up.

'I have to make water.'

'In there!' he growled angrily, pointing to a door in the wall to the west. I put on my shoes and walked over to the opening. There was no door, just a small room jutting out from the wall. Was it a latrine? I felt my way cautiously, not wanting to step into an eastern style floor-commode or, worse yet, something that would have belonged in one. There was nothing in the small cubicle, not even a drain. I looked up and realized that this cubicle was in lieu of a watchtower. There were small holes in each wall at shoulder height from which the approach to the house could be covered with a rifle. The ground dropped away steeply under the wall, making it unnecessary to build any higher.

I relieved myself and returned to my bed finding my guard squatting in the middle of the yard by his own puddle.

I tried to get to sleep again, but sleep wouldn't come. My sinuses were driving me crazy. I tried my old habit of sleeping with my forearm across my forehead. That normally worked. But sleeping in the wind isn't a normal situation. Then I remembered the wash cloth Marja-Liisa had given me as I had left the house that morning, to wipe off the sweat during the bishop's consecration. It had been a long hot summer with still no end in sight. It was in my pocket. The thieves had handed it back to me after they had emptied my pockets, taken my rings and chain with cross. The tender-hurt feeling came back to me as it had while I had clutched the cloth during my trip and mopped my face with it. It was the one thing I had left that was dear to me, dear because my wife had been thoughtful enough to remember that it would be a help to me. I spread it over my face and forehead. As long as I lay facing the wind, the wind kept it in place, but whenever I changed position it blew away. I wasn't going to get any sleep this way. Again I sat up and pushed my charpai back towards the wall, hoping to get out of the wind. My guard woke up, so I asked him for a chadar.

'There's no chadar,' came the disgruntled reply – he didn't like being woken up time and again. He got up and motioned me to follow. There were two large rooms on the north side of the courtyard. (The higher mountains encircling this projecting ridge were closest on this side.) He led me to the room in the corner of the courtyard and put me on a charpai at the back of the room, drawing a charpai in front of the door for himself so as to block the way should I think of trying to leave by that route. Here there was no wind and the cloth stayed in place. Sleep came quickly.

I felt as though I had just dropped off to sleep when I heard him telling me to get up as he stood by my side. I wondered what this was all about. Why shouldn't I get to sleep through what had been left of the night?

He led me through the courtyard and out of the door in the outer wall. The moon was already high in the sky, so I must have slept for some hours, since it had not yet risen when I fell asleep. Was he taking me outside before sunrise to 'answer the call of nature'? That was common practice, for darkness is the only privacy available in areas where there are no sanitary facilities. If that was his purpose, he was taking me to some truly remote spot! We crossed the outer yard where the cows and water buffalo were tied up, past a few olive trees, back down the track we had come up the night before, then down the steep hill past two more newly planted peach trees with troughs dug around them to catch every possible drop of water, towards the ravine at the bottom of the wadi. Here there was a dark cut in the mountainside, partly hidden by two large clumps of bunch grass. Was this the place they used? But why in the world was the man carrying chains?

Captivity

He led the way into the cut. It wasn't just a cut, it was a cave, a man-made cave. The heavy wooden lid of a large shipping crate blocked animals from entering. It had Russian lettering on it, undoubtedly a product of the war across the border in Afghanistan. The slight man heaved at the plate until he had worked it to the side, where he leaned it against the small pile of hay stored in the cave.

'Sit!' He directed me to the left side opposite the pile of hay and away from the mouth of the cave, lit a tiny kerosene light from the bottom half of a Heineken beer can and proceeded to fasten the chains around my ankles. It hadn't even occurred to me that the chains might be meant for me . . . Where in the world did that beer can come from – here in fundamentalist Islamic territory? Diplomatic rubbish in Peshawar? There was really nothing that couldn't be obtained – for a price – in this country.

'Careful, that hurts!' I said, straining to keep my ankles as wide apart as I could against the pressure of the chains to make sure of a loose fit.

'No hurt,' came the reply as if he knew better.

'What is this nonsense all about?' I protested, 'where do you think I'm going anyway? This is ridiculous!'

'Not know Urdu,' was the all too convenient reply. He walked away without a further word, leaving me sitting in the dirt, feet chained together, only the weak light from the kerosene wick for company. What was wrong with staying in the house? Was I just brought here for a while so the gang could see me without going to the house and risk being seen? First the hujra, then the house, now the cave. Just a few hours in each place. Would they keep on moving me like this? If only I never had to get back in the car and go through that again! Even when my ransom was arranged I wouldn't want to go back that way. Would they have to smuggle me back out the way they had smuggled me in? Probably, they wouldn't want to be identified. They wouldn't risk letting me be seen with them at any cost, no, going out was bound to be just as bad as coming in had been!

I couldn't believe it was happening. I felt somehow foolish. This was getting too melodramatic. It couldn't be real, no-one would ever believe me. This only happened in bad films. But the discomfort assured me that it was very real. The wall of the cave was jagged slate in clay. I couldn't lean against it, it was like so many needles pricking my skin. I sat hugging my knees until my buttocks were so numb I had to find a different position. A long, close look at the pile of hay revealed that it was so full of insects that it wasn't worth trying; I could do without the bites and the itching. I swung myself around so that I could lean against the wooden crate top. How good it felt to get some of the pressure off my backside and to be able to stretch my legs out in front of me. From here I could see out of the cave, as well as be seen by any chance passer-by. I hoped it wouldn't infuriate my guard, who had told me to sit on the other side, away from the opening. I had already annoyed him twice last night and he wasn't a particularly friendly type, but the relief was worth the risk.

The hours passed slowly. The sun had risen past the mountain ridge to the east an hour ago. It must be past eight o'clock, the shadow cast by the mouth of the cave was not quite thirty degrees. So some four hours had passed since my guard had left me. I put out the light, it was almost out of fuel anyway, and was so weak it didn't make any difference to the gloom of the cave.

Until now I had not wanted to do anything about the condition I had been left in, apart from changing my position. I had no idea when the man would return, or when the others might come and didn't want to risk giving away the fact that I could free myself. Now it seemed that no-one was coming. Outside it was light but inside the cave it was dark. If anyone should surprise me they wouldn't see me getting back into the chains so I decided to take them off for a while, just to be able to sit in a different position. I had no intention of trying to flee. In my clerical-collared shirt and trousers I would stick out like a sore thumb. Everyone would recognize me immediately as an *angrez*, a foreigner. Someone else would pick me up and ask for ransom money. The whole thing would begin all over. In order to make an escape feasible, I would need local clothing, preferably dark, so as to make moving at night easier. But where would I get that? All kinds of crazy ideas came to mind, overpowering my guard and taking his clothes, pretending to be a fakir without clothes, or just a loincloth torn from my clothing. Did fakirs ever wander off into tribal territory, or did they stay in the cities and plains? I took off my right shoe and slipped my foot, instep pressed against ankle, out of the chain. Would it be as easy to put back on? I tried it out, repeating the procedure. I could slip back into the chains in one more or less smooth movement, provided I kept them laid out in just the right fashion. Then I stood up and stretched myself, trying to get the kinks out.

I needed the lavatory. What had the guard expected me to do, do it right there where I sat – and with my feet chained together! It wasn't even possible to squat! Whatever he had thought I was slowly getting the impression that he wasn't too bright, I wasn't going to live in filth in the cave.

Three or four steps ahead was a dike piled up across the entrance to keep rain water from flowing into the cave. That would do nicely. Then I remembered the chains. If I were caught literally with my pants down, I'd better have the chains with me. I would face away from the mouth of the cave, my feet would be hidden and with my trousers around my ankles it would not be visible, whether I had the chains on or not. I could stall, pleading privacy if anyone came, and get the chains back on right there. I went to the dike where I dug a hole in the soft earth with my shoe. No-one came. What a relief! I covered the hole carefully. There were already enough flies in the cave. I didn't want any more. I went back to my place, put the chains back on and leaned against the boards. The crossboards were in just the wrong places, but it was better than the wall of the cave. I gradually moved further and further down the board looking for the least uncomfortable position. I ended up lying flat on the floor of the cave. In the dirt.

Monday 10th September, 9 a.m.

I dozed off, my tiredness overcoming my discomfort. When I awoke, I sat up again against my boards and looked down at my feet as I hugged my knees. I couldn't believe my eyes, my guard must be even more simple than I had suspected: the lock was put on the chains wrongly. I reached down and confirmed what my eyes were telling me, the hook slipped right out of the loop. If the chain had been any looser, it might even have opened on its own. In the early morning dark I hadn't been able to see it. My acrobatics in slipping out of them had been unnecessary.

I thought of Peter in prison. God had sent an angel and opened his bonds, led him past the sleeping guards and let him escape from prison. Is this what it had been like for him? Had God worked through stupid or careless guards? Miracles were miracles to those who were willing to see them as such, to others they were flukes, chance. Faith meant interpreting our lives as the result of God's guidance. Wasn't it a miracle that my car hadn't started? If it had, they might have decided that the loot had been sufficient and would have followed the suggestion of the man pulling the strings and finished me off then and there. As it was they had to keep me in order to extract a ransom. It was a real miracle that I was still alive, although the logic behind it was simple enough.

'The Lord is my shepherd . . .' Until now the twenty-third psalm had only come in bits and pieces, as my subconscious, or the Spirit, if they can be separated, had dictated. Now I began consciously to try to reconstruct the psalm, bemoaning my miserable memory. Parts that I couldn't remember at first in English after being away from Canada for twenty years came in German, the language I had studied in. Some snatches came in Finnish, the language we spoke in our home. From one language I could reconstruct another, even most of the Urdu translation I was supposed to have learned in language school.

Slowly the whole psalm took shape:

The LORD *is* my shepherd; I shall not want.

He maketh me to lie down in green pastures: he leadeth me beside the still waters.

He restoreth my soul: he leadeth me in the paths of righteousness for his name's sake.

Yea, though I walk through the valley of the shadow of death, I will fear no evil: for thou *art* with me; thy rod and thy staff they comfort me.

Captivity

Thou preparest a table before me in the presence of mine enemies: thou anointest my head with oil; my cup runneth over.

Surely goodness and mercy shall follow me all the days of my life: and I will dwell in the house of the LORD for ever.

(Psalm 23:KJV)

I felt as though the psalm had been written for me. For some years now the Bible passages I had read had held primarily an academic interest for me as a theologian. Seldom had I experienced any more that excitement one feels at understanding a new and deep truth for the first time. Very seldom, and almost exclusively when preparing for a sermon had I felt that God's word had spoken directly to me. In that sense I had been grateful for my preaching duties: they had forced me to wrestle with the texts until I heard them speak. It had been a long 'dry period' influenced by many factors, including disappointment at not having prayer answered in a vital matter. Why should I be gaining ever new insights when the basics of the Christian faith were clamouring for recognition and enactment on their own exquisitely simple level?

Jesus, with his succinct and straightforward teaching, still fascinated me. Why did we theologians have to complicate the issues – explain away the radicality of Jesus' ethic? It was ethics, wasn't it: applied Christianity, believing in Christ and eternal salvation through him without following him. Why should the rest of the Bible speak to me when I was still trying to digest the Sermon on the Mount? Now this psalm I had learned by heart as a child spoke loud and clear. It was a true source of comfort and encouragement. In our family we had learned a lot of scripture by heart, but it was this one psalm which spoke to me now.

The hours seemed endless. The sun had not yet reached its zenith, it seemed to make no progress at all. Normally days went too fast. There was no time for quiet reflection and little time for prayer. Now I had all the time in the world and nothing to distract me but myself and my predicament. Still, praying for my situation was not that easy. There was only so much to say. Praying for others: family, friends, relations, colleagues, acquaintances, former students etc. was easier and more time consuming. Our field representative, Maija-Leena Pajari, would be meeting now with the bishop at 10 a.m., 'presenting her credentials', discussing our mission's role in the church's ministry. What would they think of my disappearance? 'Lord, help them to find common ground and the right wavelength to communicate on,' I prayed.

It brought inner peace and gave a sense of meaning to my being there in the cave all alone to remember the hundreds of people who came to mind at different times and ask God for his help in their lives. There were family and friends, Pakistani colleagues, friends and contacts, students I had taught recently and as long as thirteen years earlier, childhood friends and people who had influenced my life in one way or another. Now and again my thoughts turned to myself and my own predicament. I would ask God specifically to provide a way out for me, not just wish he would do it, but ask for it. At the same time I had the distinct feeling that asking was superfluous: God was taking care of me, I didn't need to worry for myself.

What relevance had my theological studies for me in this new-found situation? The problem bothered me constantly that day. For years I had had the feeling that much of what we did at university had no relevance for life whatsoever, although it had been those studies which had equipped me to make that analysis. We had to go further, beyond the superficialities of academic infighting. Something needed to be done to make theology and the Christian faith interesting, no, captivating for our generation. I couldn't blame my contemporaries for the cynicism with which they regarded us Christians. Academic necessities required researchers to deal with ever increasingly peripheral issues. That left very little to deal with the real issues such as sin. The Christian faith needed to be made to relate to life in an holistic sense. We needed a 'Theology of Life', a theology for living. My own research had been leading me in this direction ever since as a student I had recognized that the Old Testament God was from the very beginning depicted as the 'Living God', the God of life, not some existential entity to be philosophically grasped, dissected, reassembled and described, 'labelled', so that we would know what to do about him. Dogma was never intended to be a substitute for living, experiential faith: it creates a boundary around experiential faith to guard against contradictions and separations. Heresy originally meant splitting away, division in the body of believers. Dogma was formulated to keep the church as the sum of its believers together. In academics this has been turned upside down: the teaching and research exist for the theory, for the fellowships, grants, professorships, for the renown associated with being 'the authority' on a subject. Theology should help one to experience God, to know him, it should protect the life of faith, not suffocate it. It should encourage the theologian to take his faith experientially, to do theology from within, as an expression of one's relationship with God.

Here in the cave, cut off from the rest of the world and the ivory towers of academia, I felt I was perhaps 'getting a handle on theology', understanding better the way Jesus had done it in his inimitable and unique way. That was the key to a relevant theology, it always had been: Jesus, God incarnate, God in human form, tangible, real, not some abstract idea subject to debate. I felt that I understood, having no place to sit, stand or lie in a comfortable manner how the man who had no place to lay his head had to see the theology of his day in a different light, and how, in light of him, we needed to see theology in a different light.

We tend to take the most magnificent things for granted: life itself, love, friendship, belonging, our senses and abilities. We spend our theological energies on matters of little direct consequence for our daily lives. What was the meaning of life? What was my purpose in living? Why was I here? Why was I kidnapped? The important questions were not theoretical in nature, but dealt with the basic realities in life, the ones Jesus related to.

I tried an outline in my mind, but couldn't bring it together. It was hard to concentrate. One thought would not yet be carried through when interrupted by another: are the boys at school today? How is Marja-Liisa holding up? Did she get any sleep last night? Is anyone there to help her? Who would be doing the shopping? A thought became a prayer, it too would be interrupted. There was the pain in my arm, the discomfort of the chains and the earthen floor, the memories of the attack which came rushing back time and again. Should I have resisted? Shouldn't I have stopped the car in the first place? Should I have rammed them as they were overtaking and forced them into the canal? No use thinking about that sort of thing now! I'd have to trust that my reactions had been right, after all, I couldn't change them now, and at least I was still alive!

It was no good, I needed paper and something to write with. If only I had a ball-point pen, I could write on the inside of my shirt or trousers, jot down an outline, note key ideas and phrases.

A clattering of stones outside the cave heralded a visitor. The mouth of the cave darkened and a young man entered. I had not seen him before, but he looked suspiciously like the young driver who had shown the way up here to the gang last night. Roundish face, medium dark complexion, no beard, just small moustaches, he wore the same kind of white skull cap as the driver had. Were they brothers, and had he come to keep an eye on me and my guard, to make sure he didn't let me go or sell me off to someone else? He had a small aluminium tea pot for me. He sat down and silently poured me a cup of the sweet, black tea. It was already cold, but I needed it. The first three or four little handleless cups only whetted my thirst. I ended up drinking the whole pot.

After the first few cups he started questioning me – it was the same old things: had I brothers, father, house, car, money, in short, whether I was worth the effort. He seemed straightforward in his interest, and I found myself wondering whether it was just the typical Pakistani curiosity after all and I was imagining that he was involved in the gang. At least he knew Urdu and I could communicate with him. And he was pleasant enough, didn't act or look like a crook. Should I try to sound him out on helping me to get away? I was of two minds, suspicious. I'd have to be careful not to make things worse for myself, 'wily like a serpent, but without guile like a dove . . .'

'Don't you have something for me to sit on? A charpai or something? After all, I am a human being, not an animal to be tied up like this!'

Captivity

'I am only your guest! More tea?'

'Yes please. What do you mean "my" guest – don't you live here?'

'No! I'm just visiting here.'

I decided to sound him out about food, I was going to have to get something to eat from somewhere.

'Don't these people eat breakfast?' I asked, unbelieving.

'Why, didn't they give you any breakfast?'

'Nothing all day yesterday until they brought me here, when I got an egg. Today, just a cup of tea at four o'clock in the morning. Since then this tea you brought is the first thing I've had.'

'No food all day yesterday?' he asked, astonished.

'No, nothing all day,' I repeated. He assumed a stoic, almost condescending look.

'This is a dangerous place, the men don't have time for breakfast, they have to keep moving. There are enemies, thieves. This is a backward area, tribal. Everybody has his enemies, a man has to check on his fields and animals to see that no damage has been done in the night. I'm from the city, you know, we have air conditioning, electricity, talk Urdu and everything. We're not backward like these people! Now that I'm here you won't lack anything. You'll have milk in your tea, proper food, a charpai, everything.'

It was what the gang leader had told me last night. It was almost like a recording. I would have to revise my idea of comfort to be happy about the 'encouragement' they were trying to give me. And it had that hollow ring of empty phrases that Pakistanis use to fulfil cultural obligations, the main objective being to keep a person happy. I would have to take the lead in the discussion if I wanted to find anything out:

'When did you get here?'

'Just now.'

'You mean you came all the way from the city this morning?' I tried to lead him.

'Yes, just now.'

'You must be very tired then!' I rejoined, hoping he would divulge where he had come from and how long it took.

'Well, not too bad, it's a two hour journey.'

'On foot?' My guess was right and I could hardly believe it – only a two hours' walk to civilization! From there I could catch a bus or at least make a phone call. I hid my excitement and picked up on his comment about the lawlessness of the area.

'You know there were times according to the *Taurat* (Torah) when things for God's people were like they are here, and God wasn't happy. There was no king yet in Israel and the people did as they liked until things got really bad and God had to send a *Qazi* (judge) to sort the trouble out. Things would go well until the Qazi died and then the Bible always tells us the same thing, "and the people did what was right in their own eyes." That's just like this tribal area – nobody follows the law, everybody takes the law into his own hands. There's no respect for God's commandments. There will never be any progress here, because there is no safety. That is why God gave man laws, for man's own benefit, his own safety and prosperity.'

'Things were good when the British were here,' he said with apparent nostalgia even though he had been born at least twenty-five years after the British had left India, but probably with the purpose of making me feel good. 'They made people abide by the law. Nowadays, not even the city people abide by the law.' His analysis of the cities was certainly right. Money manipulates everything in society. Right goes to the highest bidder. The poor have no refuge, certainly not in the courts at any rate.

'Which city do you live in?' I hoped he wouldn't connect this question to our earlier discussion about how long it had taken him to get here.

'Jamrud.' My heart beat faster. I wasn't in North Waziristan in the vicinity of Bannu after all! Those lights in the distance had been Jamrud, or further off, maybe even Peshawar then!

My thoughts churned, incited by the prospects of escape. I was able to get out of the chains, but would keep them on in order not to be caught without them. From here it would be possible to walk all the way home if need be, what would it be, thirty, forty, kilometres? I couldn't escape in these western clothes, clerical collar and all, but there might be a chance some time, maybe on a rainy night, when no-one would be up and about. When that chance might come, I had no idea. The weather was hot, sweltering, here in the cave just a little below body temperature, outside, by day, above it. The patch of sky I could see was the same pale, dusty blue it was seven months of the year. I had to hope for rain. The monsoon season from the middle of July to the end of August was over. That was the reason for this renewed heat wave, but sooner or later it would have to rain. That would be my chance – in a week, maybe two. Could it last months? The possibility weighed on me in its full reality, but still, the news that I might be able to get home on my own without any connivance buoyed me up.

He didn't seem to notice my excitement, had taken the questions very matter-of-fact. Best to keep up the conversation.

'Is Jamrud a big place?' I knew it to be a small city on the border of the tribal area to the government-controlled part of the Frontier Province.

'Yes, it's a big place with electric lights, schools, everything.' The concept 'big' was relative, I had to remind myself.

'Are you here staying with your sister?' He didn't like the question: had I hit on the right connection? His brother had shown the way last night to his sister's place. He got up from where he had leant back against the old hay full of bugs, collected the pot and cup and told me not to worry about anything, he would take care of me.

Monday, midday

I had been trying to trace the movement of the shadow on the wall of the entrance to the cave, cast by the sun as it fell into the cut, to keep track of the time. A clump of long bunch grass on the rim of the entrance made a good sundial. It seemed to take eternities for its shadow to pass from one prominent stone embedded in the shale and clay to another. The shadow was now perpendicular, so it was about midday.

It seemed unreal that a day has so much time in it. Where did the time go to in normal, everyday life? Would I get used to this standstill in time? Would I have to? How long would it take? Could it be true that I had been kidnapped only yesterday and had been here in the cave only eight hours?

One of the first thoughts I had after my kidnapping the day before came to mind again: 'Did this have to happen for me to get to have a rest?' I was totally exhausted from my workload. As treasurer of our Church Province I had had to share much of the responsibility for running the diocese during the past seven months of interregnum as there was no bishop present to dump the more difficult problems on: the personnel matters including, of course, the ever present disputes; dealings with local authorities and government officials; managing the handling of legal disputes and court cases in conjunction with the Diocesan Secretary; even arranging a visit by the Archbishop of Canterbury to our area.

I had, in a crazy incongruency, been almost relieved at not having to see the long day through with its long, pompous and sometimes tedious ceremonies. I had done my job in preserving the diocese through the turmoil and infighting between groups which had been struggling for power in order to be able to decide who the next bishop would be, all in spite of court orders and injunctions. Now it was the new bishop's job to get the church back on course. But by today the aspect of the rest I had fantasized about had withered. It was enough to keep one's hope in this situation.

I tried to think back to those initial minutes blindfolded in the car with the pistol to my head. How had I been able to think this might not be so bad, they would make me comfortable, give me good food to eat, maybe even try to tempt me with a girl? Fantasies were a strange thing, they surprised you when you least expected them.

I couldn't sit or lie any more. My backside and limbs had gone through innumerable cycles of pain and numbness. I unhooked the chains and stood up. It felt marvellous after the original stiffness had gone. I also had a better view out of the mouth of the cave, although I was still too far back in the cut to get a wide-angled view of the area outside, and could only see a patch of the barren mountainside and sky opposite. Without my glasses it was difficult to recognize details. I squinted hard to focus on the distant slope. On the far side of the valley, beyond a ridge dividing the wadi in two like the one this cave was situated on, it looked as if there was a small city cut into the rock about half-way up the mountainside, a little higher than I was. Without my glasses everything in the distance was blurred. Scattered along the edges of the building-like forms were small dark figures. Were they cypress trees? Were they sentinels? There was no movement as far as I could see. They could hardly be human beings out there in the direct midday sun. It was hot enough here in the cave, what must it be like out there?

The clatter of stones rolling down the hillside outside the cave woke me from my thoughts. I sat down and fumbled with the chains. I wasn't getting the hook right. A boy appeared in the cut at the mouth of the cave. Luckily the sun had not yet passed the crest of the mountain so was in his eyes and he couldn't see me working to get the chains closed in the darkness of the cave. He approached warily, waiting for his eyes to adjust to the dim light. He looked like my younger brother David, who had died twelve years ago: the same fair complexion and red hair, the same set of chin. Some Pathans were like that, but the people keeping me were much darker, with an almost Punjabi villager complexion. What was he doing here? Was he perhaps a foreigner who had been kidnapped as a child and brought up here? My mind was in a suspicious state, but kids had been abducted right off the Mall Road where we had first lived in Peshawar. This boy would be thirteen, maybe fourteen years old, but carried himself with the bearing of a man who owns the world, as only a Pathan can. He settled down on the dike of loose earth, carefully lifting the long tail of his surprisingly neat and clean kameez.

He greeted me in Pushto asking about my strength.

'By God's grace!' I answered with the common formula, but meaning it. The pleasantries continued for some time as cultural dictates required. Beyond the Islamic greetings it was difficult to communicate anything. He knew only one or two sentences of Urdu. Mostly he just sat there and stared at me, spitting the juice every now and again from the *naswaar*, a hybrid of snuff and chewing tobacco he had tucked away under his lower lip like the majority of Pathan men. He wasn't worried about anyone finding him here, he sat with composure. Had my guard sent him? Why had two different people come? Both had come straight into the cave, not just by accident. Where was my guard? It was past midday and I still hadn't received anything to eat. I decided to ask where he was.

'Bazaar kay', he replied in Pushto.

He was in the bazaar, wherever that was from here. Perhaps that was why this boy wasn't worried about being found snooping around? He tried to get something across to me, shaking his leg and motioning away from his foot and down the mountain. I should try to get my chains off and escape. He looked on in expectation, waiting to see if I could get them off. Was this a trick? Was he setting me up to see if I could get them off or not? I couldn't get anywhere in these clothes by daylight anyway, so there was no point. Better to keep it a secret that I can get loose any time I like. I shook my head as if to say 'hopeless! I can't get free!', throwing in a slightly scornful look for good measure. He got up and left with even less protocol than when he had come.

It was taking forever for the shadow on the wall of the cut to begin slanting, showing that the sun had passed its zenith. The grey-brown barren mountain opposite seemed further away than in the soft light of morning. The whitish stratum with its cubical shapes higher up the mountainside appeared still to be guarded by the dark shapes placed at intervals. Nothing was moving outside. The heat had brought the world to a standstill. It was uncommonly hot for September, and even the higher elevation did not seem to help. I suppressed a sarcastic laugh at the thought I had had some weeks earlier that this area would be a nice place to go to beat the heat in Peshawar. The porthole view out of the mouth of the cave couldn't keep my attention long, my thoughts wandered back to my family. Would they know even now? When would I get to see them again? Would it be days? Weeks? Months? I dared not even think of the prospect of years.

Could it really be that it was only yesterday that I had been kidnapped, the day before still sitting with the bishop-to-be in the chapel of the mission hospital, Peshawar, standing by him in his inner preparation for the vows he was to take and the task he was to embark on? I realized now, that it had been for my sake that I had been chosen to stand by him; I had been in need of inner preparation for this ordeal. Strange, how God had allowed this to happen, not giving any warning, but preparing me all the while, I thought. What did he plan to achieve through this? I was surprised that I didn't feel bitter, only awe-struck, surprised that this brought me closer to him, making me more dependent on him.

Again my thoughts turned into prayers: for people I had not even thought of for years, childhood friends, teachers. Pastor Don who had on the spur of the moment gone from house to house collecting donations from members of his church, packing his car with food, clothing and household goods – and his wallet with money and then driving non-stop nearly 3,200 kms in twenty-six hours to bring assistance to us when our house burned down one freezing (−20°C) morning. I had been a teenager then at home in Canada. I prayed for friends I had studied with, for colleagues I had worked with, for former students of mine, from first graders in Christian Education class to the university theology students in Tübingen. For the mentally disturbed I had counselled. For the people who had caused me trouble at various stages. For old parishioners in the three churches I had pastored in Germany. For my present colleagues in the Church of Pakistan. I was amazed at how many people's lives had crossed with mine. It had been a life rich in experience till now. Could it be that it was to end now, in this way? The words of the mobster in the car yesterday cut deep – fifteen miles into the desert and finish! – No, this couldn't be the end, they hadn't finished me off then. They were keeping me alive. This was the beginning of something new!

Monday, early afternoon

The shadow on the wall of the entrance to the cave had begun to slant away to the east. At least half a day had passed. The half-way mark was important. From here on it was downhill, even though the hours seemed to get longer as the day passed. The pain in my buttocks was excruciating. There were only a couple of sitting positions. As long as I didn't move, my back was alright, but every movement with my right arm was agonizing. I had to look forward to nightfall. That would mean another day had passed.

Someone was coming. The tell-tale rattle of stones rolling down the hillside was an early-warning signal. I checked to see that the chains were all right. Nothing happened. Again the sound of stones rolling, but no-one entered the cave. The situation made me tense. Let whoever was coming come, but I didn't like this suspense. After a few minutes stones fell over the mouth of the cave into the cut. Then the visitor became visible. From behind one of the large clumps of bunch grass growing along the edge of the cut a *koh* (lizard) appeared. The reptile was about sixty centimetres long, a yellowish light grey-brown. It struggled to cross the cut above the mouth of the cave and while traversing the stretch lost its foothold and dropped the three metres to the floor of the cut landing on its belly with a thud and facing me directly from little more than a metre's distance. Did these things bite, I wondered, perturbed, looking at the huge lizard. It lay motionless for a few minutes taking me in. I made a quick movement and it turned immediately, waddling away as quickly as the clumsy animal could.

Quiet returned to the cave, and with it my preoccupation with my situation. The men would be returning tonight and would be able to tell me what the arrangements would be for me after having phoned St John's Cathedral School. It would be a consolation to know that Marja-Liisa knew I was alive and well. It was even worse for them than for me. At least I knew what had happened to me. Besides, the worst danger, the critical phase when they had made up their minds what to do with me, had passed. I hoped that the rest would just be waiting until I got a chance to escape. At least I knew now that I was within walking distance of civilization. There was a way out. It was do-able.

What would my wife be going through there at our home in the Cantonment? I could visualize her sitting by the door on the low divan with Anna on her lap, the boys nervously fidgeting around, desperate, not knowing what to make of it all. At the door – yes, they were waiting for me to come, or even to have a piece of news. The living room was dark in my mind, not only because the windows were shaded by cane blinds to keep out at least some of the intense heat. There was an inherent darkness, the patches of wall where the paint had fallen off due to the salinity in the brickwork only emphasized it. In my mind's eye I saw a picture of hopelessness. It wrenched my heart to see it, but I was thankful that I could at least picture them in my mind.

Could they even picture where I was? Were they alone like that, totally abject? How would they cope? Who would go out to the bazaar and haggle with the shopkeepers for the vegetables, buy fruit, meat? Who would go to the bakery to buy milk, yoghurt, butter, bread? Who would take the boys to school? Had they gone to school today? 'Lord, stand by them as you are standing by me!' I prayed. Again I was jerked from my thoughts by the sound of rolling pebbles outside the cave. Then came footsteps. My guard had come.

He was in a sombre mood, didn't even glance at me. Instead, he stooped for the *lota* and filled the tiny cup, placing it on the ground. He turned towards me and squatted, opening the chadar he had wrapped up under his arm. He took a bubble-pack of pills out of its folds and popped them out one by one onto his palm. As the pile grew, so did my alarm. Frantically, I tried to think – couldn't recognize the packaging of the pills. Was it a tranquillizer? Was he going to drug me? I could stand the discomfort and the chains, but I couldn't stand the thought of having my mental faculties taken from me! I hadn't been a difficult prisoner for him, why would he want to put me to sleep? Should I overpower him and force him to take the pills? It wouldn't be any problem, his gun was in the corner behind him; I could get to him before he got to it, one lunge would do it. The chains . . . No, even with the chains I could do it, I was bigger and stronger than he. Something held me back.

Until now I had not fought back, instinctively, because of ingrained conviction. The last time I had physically beaten up someone was when I was twelve. I had cried afterwards. I couldn't do it now,

although it would have been possible. I was being held back inside. H
picked up the cup of water and I opened my mouth to protest, bu
time, but before I could speak he swallowed the whole handful of pil
himself! It was then I noticed the cotton wool in his right ear. He ha
an earache!

'When did the pain in your ear start?' I asked, wondering whethe
the overdose of whatever he had taken would help.

'This morning,' he replied, cradling his head in his hand. I couldn
help thinking, 'Serves you right,' feeling just a little ashamed at th
same time for thinking it. I couldn't shake off the feeling that he had
because of me, or better, because he was doing something he knew t
be wrong. I wanted to exploit that, both for my own and his sake.

'You know this is a bad business . . .'

There was no reply. The man sat there in his pain. No wonder h
was in a sombre mood!

'It's wrong for you to be doing this, you should let me go.'

There was still no reply.

'You know that God sees what you are up to, even though you ca
hide me from people's sight.'

The silence hung heavy in the air. He got up and told me to mov
back to the other side of the cave up against the wall and away fror
the entrance where I could be seen by a chance passer-by.

He opened my chains. It seemed to puzzle him, but he got the loc
undone. I worried about whether he would put them back on an
whether I would be able to open them anymore. Had I missed m
only chance to get out of the chains and run away? I had assumed tha
they were on for good, and that since he had hooked the loc
wrongly, I would be able to get out of them whenever I wanted. Wha
if he put them back on properly this time? For that too, I would ju
have to have faith, that my chance would come.

'Don't worry, the men will come tonight and bring news abou
you.' He unravelled his chadar more while I shifted over to the othe
side and he pulled out half of a flat bread of the type eaten with currie
by most peoples in the subcontinent. It was the same as he had give
me last night.

Captivity

'You've been to the bazaar for the medicine?' I ventured and got a nod. 'Is it far?' I wondered aloud, calculating that he had been gone all morning. The bread was probably what was left of his provisions for the trip. Being sick he wouldn't have had an appetite. I was starving. No food all day so far and only that one meal yesterday. The bread tasted delicious. I was amazed at how wonderful plain bread tastes when one is hungry.

Would it be bread and water for me from now on? Anything would do, as long as I have something to keep my strength up, I tried to reason with myself. My guard was looking around the cave for something without success. He had pulled a small red onion out of his chadar and was trying to peel it with his thumb-nail, again without any luck. Then he came up with a solution. Bending down, he put the onion on the lid of the small aluminium tea pot and whacked it with the heel of his hand, cracking it open. It split down the middle and he pulled the two halves apart. He seemed pleased with himself as he handed it to me motioning to pull out the layers beginning at the centre. The onion was warm, as if it had been in the hot sun. Who knew where he got it?

It was a meal, that was the important thing. After just a few mouthfuls, I noticed that my stomach had shrunk. I couldn't eat any more. I stood up to see if the food would settle. He didn't stop me, so I walked back and forth the three paces across my 'cell'. He motioned me to move farther back in the cave. I protested that I couldn't stand up straight there anymore. We compromised half way.

I stopped eating and stretched my limbs, trying to get my circulation going again.

'Eat up! You've got to eat a lot of bread!' He admonished me. I hung on to the piece of bread.

'I'll eat it, slowly – not to worry!'

'Sit!' He pointed for me to sit down again against the wall. He got the chains and was studying how to hook them together properly. I sat down and put my feet together as I had the first time, keeping tension on the chain to make for a looser fit. He pulled at my feet and told me to put them out straight in front of me.

'This really isn't necessary!' I remonstrated with him. 'You don
need to put chains on me! Where will I go from here?'

'Need to!' he replied curtly as he worked on fixing the padlock. H
seemed intent on getting it right this time. Had he noticed that he ha
done it up wrong?

I decided that this was as good a time as any to go on the offensiv
and try to get at least a little relief from the discomforts of the cave.

'Am I an animal that you keep me tied up like this in a cave wit
not so much as a charpai to sit on? What have I done to you t
deserve such treatment? Am I not a human being? You Muslim
believe that all people are equal in God's sight, why do you keep m
as if I was some buffalo?' The accusation hit home. He gave me hi
chadar to sit on and hurriedly got up to leave, picking up the teapo
and his rifle.

'Tea, four o'clock', he announced and sauntered out into th
scorching sun. He paused at the entrance and looked carefully in a
directions before leaving the shelter of the cut and striding up the sid
of the mountain to the left of the opening.

Four o'clock, that could only be a couple of hours off, I reflected
hoping that it would help the day to go faster having only a relativel
short wait until my tea would come. How luxurious it felt to have th
thin grey sheet spread out under me. It didn't do anything to softe
the ground, but not to have to sit in the dirt did wonders for m
composure. It was a piece of civilization, culture, it gave some dignit
to my undignified position.

I checked my chains. They were tighter, but I could still slip on
foot out if I took off my shoes and socks. I took a second look an
couldn't believe my eyes: they were done up the same way as before
with the padlock on the hook and the eye, so the hook could b
undone without opening the lock! I marvelled at his stupidity. To d
it once in the darkness of night is one thing, to do it in the light of da
was too much for me. It couldn't even be explained by the amount o
pills he had taken. They were probably antibiotics that should hav
lasted him for a week to ten days. Whatever it was, the medicin
hadn't had time to take any effect yet.

Captivity

Now that I had the chadar to sit on, I experimented with new positions. The best was achieved by slipping the chains off, then slipping them back on with my ankles crossed: that way I could both extend my legs and also sit cross-legged. Praise God for small mercies, I thought. Having found a better sitting posture, my thoughts returned. Would the desperados get here before or after dark? Probably after, so as not to be seen. On the other hand they might not want to raise suspicion by coming later at night. Perhaps they would try to arrive at dusk. What news would they bring? If only I could get back quickly, before people began to get desperate or give up hope – or even manage to pay a ransom.

I couldn't digest the thought of these crooks getting their hands on money given by people for God's work. On the other hand, I had to admit to myself that sometimes God did see fit to allow money for his work to be wasted. I'd seen it happen . . . he was certainly not dependent on our money. Neither should we be.

Was I here as a casualty of Third World resentment towards the decadent-rich West, or because as a westerner I represented to them the Christian enemy of Islam? They had told me that they had wanted an American, because then the government would pay a heavy ransom to avoid an international incident. My gut feeling told me that I represented capital to them, that was why they had taken me. Yet how could a ten-year-old car represent riches to them? Maybe they had just acted on impulse. Anyway, what mattered more was why God had allowed this to happen. Would I ever find out?

I was confounded by how long a day is when one is bound and in solitary confinement. I had lots of time to pray, for anyone and everyone. Again I tried to organize my time by following what my family would be doing, praying for strength for them in this situation. Would they even be in Pakistan anymore, or would our mission have called them to Finland to await the outcome? What would I have done, if the decision had been mine to take? I would have sent the dependents home where they would be properly cared for and counselled, out of danger of reprisals if anything went wrong. Of course it would mean being cut off from developments. Would

Marja-Liisa go? Probably not, not right away, anyway. If only I knew how she and the kids were taking it!

I still had what was left of my piece of bread in my hand. It would be best to save it, I had no idea when the next piece would come, would have to make it last, ration it. If I got a chance to escape I could take it with me so I wouldn't need to expose my identity to anyone by asking for food. It would have to be kept secret that I was hamstering food. My guard would get suspicious otherwise. The haystack would do. I lifted a layer of hay and pushed the piece of bread into the depression, carefully replacing the hay. No-one would guess that anything was hidden there. Satisfied, I spread the sheet out to its full dimensions and lay down diagonally across it. Using my shoes as a pillow off the corner of the cloth, it was just large enough for me. Not even my feet had to be in the dirt. Things were getting better!

I hadn't noticed how tired I was after the exhausting day yesterday and the short night. I had got up around 4 a.m. Sleep too, would help the time to pass. Towards evening I woke up at the sound of someone approaching. It was the young man from the city bringing some tea. It was the dregs of the pot left over from someone else, cold, but it would give some energy. He wasn't very talkative, looked nervous. Perhaps he didn't get along with my guard, who obviously had a very general notion of what four o'clock meant, the sun was already about to set, the entrance of the cave in complete shadow. I drank the tepid tea straining it through my teeth and spitting out the leaves in good Pakistani fashion. The floor was there to be spit on, swept up, only this floor would never see a broom. After the liquid had seeped into the ground, the tea leaves blended in with the rest of the straw, leaves, rocks and sticks on the ground.

The time dragged on till sunset. I wondered what it would be like to spend the night in the cave. No-one had brought me food, nor had my kidnappers shown up. Was it going to be one piece of bread and an onion per day from now on? I was glad that I had hidden what was left of the bread in the hay.

Lying there I wondered what would come next. First I had been taken to the homes of the big-time crooks, then to the hujra, yesterday

Captivity

evening to the house and this morning to the cave. Was this to be the final place of confinement? There had always been new surprises. Nothing had gone according to what the crook had told me. No charpai, no food, a poor excuse for tea, no freedom to move about. On a day like this I didn't even have the chance to learn any Pushto. That way I could have at least made use of the time. Then again, maybe the time for reflection and prayer was what I needed.

An hour after dark I heard the clatter of stones again outside the cave and my guard returned. He took off my chains, picked up the teapot and lota and led the way outside. He carried the chains close by his side and motioned for me to wrap up in the chadar so no chance passer-by would see my European clothes. After leaving I realized that I had forgotten the piece of bread. Where was he taking me? Would I have to wait as long there for my next meal?

I tried to look at the surroundings, get my bearings. Not much was visible. The city lights were to the south. That was my direction. He led me back up the mountainside by a zigzag course, apparently to the house. We came to the track and were moving slowly along the ridge the houses were perched on. Suddenly he stopped in his tracks and motioned me to do the same. He had seen someone move across the ridge we were following. The shadow did not alter its course and was gone as fast as it had come, so he motioned me to follow again. This time the door was open and we stepped quickly into the courtyard where I had spent the last night.

He took me straight across the stamped mud yard past the newly planted peach tree and into the room where he had put me last night after I had asked for something to cover me against the wind. Tonight there was no wind and I had the chadar. It would have been so much more pleasant to sleep outside than in the stuffy stone structure with no windows. Besides, there would have been one hurdle less if the chance came to escape . . . But he was not to be moved.

'Sit!' He motioned to the charpai meaning for me to lie down: 'make rest!' Was he going to leave me alone to sleep here? He was back in a minute with food.

'Can you give me some water please?' He groped around in the darkness of the room until he found the lota near the door. He gave it to me and left, closing and locking the door behind him.

There was no cup, I would have to do as I had seen labourers doing, holding their heads back and pouring from the spout into their open mouths. Most important, I could wash my hands and face. The cool water wrought a cleansing I wouldn't have thought possible. I washed all the way up past my elbows like a Muslim before prayers, washed my neck under my collar before turning to the food.

In the darkness I couldn't see my food, so I ate by feel, breaking off a piece of the bread and using it to pick up the food in Pakistani fashion. With the home-made flat bread was a small steel-sheet bowl of boiled potatoes with two red chillies in a thin soup. First thing after giving heartfelt thanks, was to take half the bread and hide it in my chadar. There was plenty of it, and he would expect me to eat the lot. Obviously these people didn't have a particularly developed culinary culture. In contrast to the varied and tasty dishes common to even the simplest of homes in the Punjab and other areas of Pakistan, the food didn't taste like anything in particular except chillies, but it was nourishing and the bread was very good and satisfying. Again I ate slowly, keeping myself from wolfing it down, knowing that I would be able to eat less if I did.

When I had had enough, I lay down, using the chadar with the bread in it as a pillow – how good it felt to have the charpai to lie on.

The door opened and he was back with a lantern and the chains. He grabbed my foot and put it up against the legpost.

'There really is no need for this!' I protested.

'Need to!' came the standard reply. No use crossing him, I thought, seeing that he wasn't in a mood to discuss it; maybe his earache still bothered him.

'How is your ear feeling?'

'Better.' My man wasn't a great talker.

'Where are the men who were supposed to come?' I wondered if they had been here while I was still in the cave.

'Not know, tomorrow.' He was wrapping the chains around my leg, binding them to the frame of the string bed.

Captivity

'Not so tight, how will I be able to sleep?' I protested.

'Not tight.' It was hopeless. At least I would be able to make them looser by pushing them from my calf down around my ankle.

While there was light from the lantern I looked around the room. The walls had mud plaster in parts and there were five or six string beds standing in the middle of the room or upended against the wall. It wasn't a small room, maybe five metres square. The low roof was held up by two poles in the centre of the room, which in turn supported crossbeams that supported branches of trees. On top of these was matting. From the outside there would be ten centimetres of mud and mud plaster on top. The roof was black, as were the upper parts of the walls. They must burn fires here in the winter. I couldn't make out any chimney.

He finished with the lock and left, taking the lantern with him. What time would it be now, nine o'clock? I heard him pull his charpai in front of the door. There would be no way out tonight. I shifted around looking for the best position to lie with one leg tied up. There were no other real possibilities than the way he tied me. I worked on the chains. They came off and made it much more comfortable, but what would happen if he found me asleep without them? Last night I had woken to find him standing over me telling me to get up. Better to put them back on and keep it secret that I can get out of them. Let him think I was safely tied up. Perhaps he would get lax. That may make him slip and give me a chance. I'd have to try to sleep like this. My tiredness came to my assistance, and by lying diagonally I could get my calf directly over the frame I was tied to, lessening the tension on the chains.

This would be the second night for Marja-Liisa and the kids, would they get any sleep? Would their fears and desperation be magnified in the loneliness of the dark? Or would the stress be so heavy that they would feel drugged? Lord, help them to get the rest they need too! Sleep came quickly for me.

Tuesday 11th September, 4 a.m.

This time I heard him coming. I propped myself up on my elbow and pushed my leg tighter down into the chains. If he hadn't noticed that they would be loose around the ankle when he did them up, he wouldn't notice now either. Let him think he had me secured.

He fumbled with the lock on the chains in the dark until he got it open.

'Uttho - Get up!' It was one of those perfunctory two-syllable sentences of his I would just have to get used to.

'I need a drink of water,' I said in the more straightforward way of the subcontinent. One didn't dwell on formalities of etiquette in these matters. He fished around in the dark by the door for the lota. I drank and splashed a handful of water on my face. I noticed that he had a reed mat rolled up under his arm. They were used as outdoor prayer mats and general purpose mats by villagers and poor city dwellers. If only it was for me to sit on! It would change things so much! Having the chadar was great, but it didn't make the ground any flatter or take any bumps and lumps out of the gravel and rocks on the floor of the cave. A stiff mat like that one made of split reeds would be a giant step up on the ladder of creature comforts.

While he unbolted the courtyard door I marvelled again at the brightness of the moonlit sky. Orion was low in the sky, much lower than I would have expected. But how was I to know what to expect? The last time I had really paid any attention to the constellations was more than twenty years ago in Canada! I would lie on the roof of our house and watch the stars. I would need to get my bearings by the stars if I were going to travel by night.

I had become much more conscious of direction since coming to Pakistan in February 1986. In Islamic society the *qibla*, or direction of Mecca plays an important role. People perform the *namaaz* or *salaat* (prayers) five times a day in that direction. The mosques and prayer platforms are marked for that purpose with the *mithrab*, which shows the *qibla*. Graves are laid out from north to south, so that the face turned to the right in death will be found in constant prayer

Captivity

and the *qibla* will not be desecrated by feet stretched out toward it.

More important, in a country unblessed by sanitary facilities, one needed to be careful not to face toward or away from the *qibla* when relieving oneself. People would be very offended if they noticed one doing otherwise, and there is nothing like a religious insult to infuriate a Muslim and whip up a civil disturbance. Direction was important for purely secular reasons as well. While planning the school and other buildings with builders and architects, I had learned that the primary concern in construction at these latitudes was to create a minimum of wall space that would have no shade from the sun. Long, narrow buildings were built east to west with a veranda on the long south face and ventilators high in the wall on the north side or back of the building. This applied, of course, only where there were no buildings surrounding and providing shelter.

The slight man led me out through the small doorway across the level space on top of the ridge. Huddled up against the wall a water buffalo was sleeping and across the yard I could see the shapes of some small cows, kept by people in areas where there was limited fodder, under a thorn tree.

As we moved on, I noticed that he was leading me off towards the other side of the ridge. Here, I could hear the sound of running water down in the valley. Would he be taking me down there to some new hiding place? If it were only somewhere near that stream I could hear, then I could wash, maybe even bathe! I soon lost hope of that, for as we walked along the side of the stony ridge we began to climb away from the sound of water.

The path led past the ruins of a stone tower. All the Pathan houses have one, complete with firing slits in the masonry for them to protect their homes from attack. Feuds are very much a part of their life. Male cousins are often bitter enemies, partly because of inheritances, partly because they marry first cousins, and while they don't treat their wives particularly well, they don't like to see their sisters treated poorly by their cousins who married them.

Perhaps someone had begun to build a house here and never finished. There were also a few graves, elongated piles of stones, as we breasted the ridge. A fresh breeze caught my hair and the chadar. It was so invigorating and refreshing to be able to move about and feel the caress of the wind on my skin. Tied up in the cave with not so much as a breath of wind was nothing to look forward to. I hoped this would be better. At least I was likely to have the mat he was carrying.

We doubled back on the other side of the ridge in the direction of the cave. It was going to be the same thing again today after all. Well, the advantage was that I knew where I was going and what it would be like. With the mat it would be all right. The clatter of the stones dislodged by our feet as we clambered down the hillside seemed deafening in the stillness of the early morning night.

The track that led up to the house from the valley lay just below us. My guard stepped across it and in a single, totally fluid movement stopped, squatted and motioned me to do the same. There was something animal about him I had never seen in a person before. What had he smelt or heard? His reaction had been apparently instinctive, honed into him by the constant feuding and lawlessness of the tribal territory. He crouched with his chin pulled down against his chest hiding his face. In the dark he would look like just another of the boulders strewn across the mountainside, even from a short distance. Anyone not expecting to see a person would simply walk past without noticing.

Slowly he lifted his head. Then, craning his neck to see down the mountainside, studied the panorama closely for some minutes before standing up as unceremoniously as he had squatted. He led the way on past the two young peach trees planted in large depressions that collected rainwater and onward to the cave.

In the cave it was hot and humid compared with the cool night air. It was pitch black. He hadn't bothered to bring the Heineken beer-can-lamp this time. Wherever in the world had he obtained that lamp in a country as 'dry' as Pakistan! The people who make their meagre living sifting through and recycling rubbish must have found it in some diplomat's dustbin and sold it for a couple of pennies to someone who had cut it in half, fitted a lid on it and added a wick. He unrolled the reed mat in the place where he had made me sit the day before.

Captivity

'Sit!' He pointed to the mat and pouring me a cup of tea admonished me to drink it.

This time the tea was hot and fresh. Things looked a little brighter with this and a proper mat to sit on, even though I was back in the cave. I had several small cups while he stood at the entrance studying the canyon. At least he wasn't carrying his kalashnikov. Maybe my cooperation had satisfied him that I wouldn't make any trouble.

'Ajjilabad, dayr khatrnaak, aadmi margiya.' I couldn't make out the first word, 'place of – "ajjil"?', but the rest, though a mix of Pushto and bad Urdu, was clear, 'very dangerous, man died'. Was that why he was studying the scenery so carefully? Had someone been shot yesterday? Was he expecting trouble? Why, then, wasn't he carrying his assault rifle? Was he just trying to impress on me the danger of trying to escape? Who was to know? He fixed the chains again, things were becoming routine.

The silence of the pre-dawn night before the world awoke was intensified by the isolation of the cave. The infinitesimal noises of insects in the haystack filled the hollow cavity like the resonance body of a musical instrument. Were they busy on the bread I had hidden there? There was a much louder noise as something pushed out through the hay. The sky was beginning to grey opposite the cave and I could make out movements at the edge of the pile. A small shape darted across the space between the hay and my mat, diving under the curled-up-corner. I struck out by reflex more than anything else and a mouse or a small rat squealed and flip-flopped over to the far corner, where it buried itself in the dry grass.

I hoped I hadn't hurt it badly: the last thing I needed here was a rotting animal stashed away in the haystack! I couldn't help thinking what Albert Schweitzer would have said . . . he detested even killing insects! Why should I think of that now? Didn't I have enough to worry about? One needed to see things in proportion and in perspective! Still, I felt bad about squashing the rodent. Did I feel sympathy for it? Had I seen myself in its place? It wouldn't do for a victim of brutality and violence to be violent.

My stomach brought my thoughts back to the bread. It was right there where I had hidden it. Putting it up close to my eyes to see it clearly I noticed that it was teeming with small, grey, multi-legged insects. They hadn't been able to do too much damage to the substance yet, so I shook them off and tried a bit, avoiding the chewed-up edge where the mouse had obviously been at work. I decided that if I hadn't become ill yet from the muddy-tasting water, the bugs wouldn't do me any harm.

It was strange, normally I got a stomach upset from practically looking at unboiled water, but I hadn't had any problems yet. The bread surprised me, it was remarkably edible! Maybe the residual moisture in the hay kept it from drying out, and of course this bread didn't have any soda in it like the stuff available in all the bazaars of Pakistan. That *naan* is delicious when warm, but gets tough as leather and then hard as rocks as it cools off and dries out. I rationed myself to a small piece, just in case there would be no food today.

I wanted to have a reserve for my escape. Would today bring a chance? Somehow I felt that there would have to be a decision soon, either escape or ransom. The crisis seemed to me to have reached a climax. Two full days had gone by and nothing had happened to bring about a change in my situation, my second day in the cave was beginning. After the total uncertainty and constant changes of the first day, this was already beginning to feel like routine. Why shouldn't it go on for two more days, even two weeks? How would I, or my family, manage that? I wasn't mentally prepared to accept that possibility.

Outside, in another world, the sun was rising. The salmon sky paled to peach before the yellow light of the first rays breached the mountain peaks and played on the terracotta walls and roof of the cave's entrance. In the golden light of dawn the earthen colours were rich and deep: reds, sienna, burnt sienna, orange, ochre. The beauty of common adobe earth was exhilarating. In just as few minutes as it had come to wonderfully colourful life, it would be flat reddish brown with a tinge of grey, but for the moment it was lovely as the mosquitos and gnats danced across its surface looking for a place to alight. Music came to mind:

Captivity

When morning gilds the skies
My heart awakening cries
May Jesus Christ be praised!
Alike at work and prayer
To Jesus I repair;
May Jesus Christ be praised!

Does sadness fill my mind?
A solace here I find,
May Jesus Christ be praised!
Or fades my earthly bliss?
My comfort still is this:
May Jesus Christ be praised!

The night becomes as day
When from the heart we say:
May Jesus Christ be praised!
The powers of darkness fear
When this sweet chant they hear:
May Jesus Christ be praised!

Be this while life is mine
My canticle divine:
May Jesus Christ be praised!
Be this the eternal song
Through ages all along:
May Jesus Christ be praised!
(Edward Caswall)

At first it felt foolish to sing aloud, but after getting over the initial inhibition, it was a liberating experience. It reminded me of how Paul and Silas in their chains in the jail at Philippi had been encouraged by singing hymns in the middle of the night. I remembered how they had been miraculously set free through an earthquake. Would God do something out of the ordinary to free me? Were the loose chains already that miracle I was waiting for? How could I just walk off into tribal territory in western dress and in broad daylight? I would need a bigger miracle.

Other morning hymns came to mind.

> Great is thy faithfulness, O God my father,
> Morning by morning new mercies I see,
> Thou changest not, thy compassions they fail not,
> Great is thy faithfulness, Lord unto me.
>
> (T. O. Chisholm)

Each had its own consolation, its own beauty, its own majesty and praise, its own influence on my mind, its own memories. In particular, the primary school children I had taught religious education in the German school system and taught these German hymns to, came to mind. True, my life had its own severe delimitations, but the sun shone across the borders confining me with the same heartening, pleasant light it did elsewhere. To see the countenance of God's blessing, the uncreated source of Light in the darkness of my cave! Yes, I felt God's mercies anew each morning: I was alive, was that not much more than all my needs?

It was self-evident to me that most of the things we worry about are really unimportant when faced with the question of life and death. If only I could concentrate on what is really important and essential in my life. How much time did I spend in my work as an administrator with the Church of Pakistan, Peshawar Diocese, doing things practically anyone with a little knowledge of bookkeeping and a sense of honesty could do, but robbing me of the time needed for essential tasks in the education of the church. The dilemma was that the local church had requested me to take on those responsibilities, it had been their priority. Modern missionaries wanted to do the things they were asked to do, the things that were a priority to the local church, whatever their own priorities were. Most ended up making compromises.

I knew I would have to delegate more and withdraw from the administrative post as soon as possible, if I got out of this. I had fulfilled the task asked of me in the interim period. It wouldn't be easy, with all the competition and infighting. It was so easy to remain dependent on outside help. Nothing would have to change in people's thoughts and behaviour as long as missionaries could be counted on to guarantee financial stability in the church. There would be no need to assume responsibility for the future of the church, no need to be accountable for the present situation.

I was conscious too, of how difficult it is for people to give up positions of power, conscious of how some people thought that it was for status and power that I had taken on the job of diocesan treasurer in the first place. When I had tried to get my Pakistani colleagues to look for a Pakistani replacement for me, they thought I had been insulted or otherwise had my feathers ruffled and needed to have them smoothed down. Even Marja-Liisa suspected my motives.

I realized, however, that true influence in a constructive sense could not be wielded from a position of power and temporal authority in the echelons of the church hierarchy. That was why I had agreed to the task only on a temporary basis until a new church leadership could be elected and established. The status quo needed to be maintained until the church as a whole knew where it wanted to go or was in a position to go through that decision-making process as a body. Otherwise the most unscrupulous and most hungry for position and power would walk all over those who simply wanted to serve. Structures and positions of authority were necessary for that. They were not necessarily the positions from which actual change and progress in the Christian community would take place. Hierarchy was inherently the servant of conservatism and the lackey of the status quo. Similarly, true authority was something no-one ever inherited with a job or position. Real authority, that held up behind one's back too, was inherently personal. It had to be earned. The hard way . . . If our goal as missionaries was to liberate people through the gospel truth about themselves and God, it had to be communicated in both a convincing and authoritative manner. The truth would only make people free if it were communicated from a position they were free to accept or reject. No matter how sincere I was, as long as I was speaking with official standing, people would think I was speaking in my own interest or because it was 'my job' to do so.

Escape from terror

I prayed for children I had taught and for many others I hadn't even thought of for years. It gave me a sense of accomplishment – that the time here in the cave was not wasted. Maybe I just needed to feel useful in some way, being taken so totally out of action.

Always the question 'Why?' lingered, not with any bitterness, but a gnawing desire to know what this was all about. While singing and praying I was at ease. I felt that there must be others praying for me as well, how else could I be coping?

I dug the bread out of its hiding place and nibbled some more. It was pleasing to have my own little secret, a feeling of independence and security, little as it was. Sitting on the reed mat felt good in comparison to the sheet and outright luxurious in contrast to sitting on the bare ground, but after a while the sore spots were back again with a vengeance. I tried to find a better position. The chains were again loose enough for me to slip out of them. By slipping my right foot back in over the left I could sit cross-legged with much less discomfort and still keep the chains on, should anyone surprise me from below, where I might not hear them approach.

Sitting like that I found that it distributed my weight over a greater area, bringing marked relief – again, at least, for a time. As the morning dragged on, I found that it was also easier to lie stretched out to full length with my feet crossed in the chains. The mat was a little small, smaller even than the chadar. As before, if I lay diagonally and used my shoes as a pillow, but now with the chadar rolled up on top of them, I was able to maintain that so important aura of humanity and self-respect that stemmed from not lying in the dirt.

I dozed off to awake to the clatter of someone coming. How long had I slept? It was the redheaded boy who had sauntered into the cave the day before. I couldn't get over how much he looked like my brother David. How would Mum and Dad take it if they were to lose me like they did David twelve years earlier? It had been bad enough that he died at the age of twenty-four when his car had skidded off the road and plunged into the river over a hundred metres below. Worse was the insecurity of his being missing for ten days before his body was found almost a hundred kilometres down-stream. Would they have already heard of my disappearance? How much would they have to bear?

The boy repeated the greetings of the day before as he squatted next to the opening of the cave and spat out the tobacco juice of his *naswaar*. He seemed content just to sit there watching me. I tried to start a conversation but with his very limited Urdu and my even worse Pushto, it wasn't easy. Mostly he spoke to me in Pushto and I to him in Urdu. I learned that he worked for my captor on daily wages digging up rocks for building a wall and transporting them to the construction site. It was pretty hard work for a thirteen year old. He must have been tougher than his slight form would have made one think.

'Where do you live?' I ventured. All I got was a blank look.

'Where is your house, if you just come here to work every day?' He raised his chin over to his right shoulder indicating that he lived up the mountain to the south-west.

'Do you have a long way to walk every day?'

'One hour – two hour,' he responded.

'Afghanistan is that way?' I sought to get confirmation that I had my bearings right. He nodded in affirmation.

'Is there a road?'

'By foot,' came the accustomed bisyllabic reply. He seemed content just to watch me, trying to figure me out.

'How far is it?'

'Twenty kilometres.'

'Do people travel this way?'

'On foot.' I wondered whether this valley was one of the many routes used for smuggling between Afghanistan and Pakistan, a major source of income for the Pathans. Drugs and weapons going both ways, electronics and other Japanese consumer goods routed with illicit money through Afghanistan, car parts and accessories, even whole engines, came into Pakistan without customs duty and sales tax. Food, especially meat on the hoof, went this route from Pakistan to Afghanistan. Camels, oxen, refrigerators, air-conditioners, washing machines, heroin, hashish, car batteries, car lubricants, cloth, glassware, everything imaginable travelled across the infamous 'Durand Line' separating the Pathans of Afghanistan and their relatives of the Tribal Territory on the Pakistani side. At Torkham the border was actually painted all the way up to the sheer rock mountainside as a white line.

'You, Muslim?' he asked abruptly.

'No, I'm a Christian.' He looked even blanker than before.

'I'm a follower of the Messiah,' I put it in words he as a Muslim might better understand.

'Isai?' He made sure I meant Jesus — Isa'al-Masih. I nodded in confirmation. It only seemed to confuse him more. Pathans refer to the scheduled castes and casteless ethnic groups who converted to Christianity at the end of the last century as 'Isai' and understand it to mean a 'black-skinned sweeper' more than a religious epithet.

He spat absent-mindedly trying to put it together.

'You're a Punjabi?' He couldn't hold himself back from asking, although it had to be obvious to even the most ignorant of backwoods Pathans that I was not.

'I work with Punjabi Christians, but not all Christians are Punjabis!'

'No?' He looked incredulous, the only 'Isai' he had ever heard of were.

'No indeed! Most *farangi* (I was conscious of using the term 'Franks' for 'European,' an inheritance of the crusades in the Islamic diction of Urdu, Pushto, Arabic, and Farsi) are either Christians or come from a Christian background. It's like you Muslims here. Everybody claims to be one, but few live like a Muslim should. It's comparable in Europe and the West. Few live like Christ or like he said we should.'

He was out of his depth. I felt sorry that we couldn't really communicate. I tried sounding him out on various Pushto words. I hadn't got very far with my guard, perhaps it would be better with him. I pointed to the haystack, asking for the word in Pushto. It took him a while to catch on, finally he said something I tried to repeat after him. I took one blade of grass and asked the word as I had heard it, but he had a different word for it. This wasn't going to be easy. 'Stone' and 'earth/dirt' were easier, but he really wasn't interested. I wondered whether I should try using him to get me a chance to bathe. I was filthy with forty-eight hours of sweat and grime from alternately sitting and lying in the dirt. Even on a normal day in Pakistan one gets amazingly dirty just from the dust in the air. The river or stream had been on my mind since I heard its rushing in the darkness that morning.

'Take me to the river so I can wash!' I tried to move him.

Amazed, he lifted his thumbs to his earlobes in imitation of the Muslim call to prayer that is sounded five times each day: at *Fajr* an hour before sunrise; at *Zohr* an hour after the sun reaches its zenith; at *Asr* two hours before sunset, at *Maghrib* or sunset and at *Isha* about two hours after sunset at these latitudes. Actually, the times were determined by the length of the shadow cast or the amount of light present in the case of the first and last prayers of the day.

'No, I don't need it for ablutions in preparation for prayers – I've been praying here already the whole time as it is, we Christians are not required to wash before praying, only a clean heart is necessary. We can pray any time, anywhere. But I feel awful, I need to bathe. There is a river over on the other side of this ridge, you can take me there!'

'Tell the man, I'm just a guest,' he said as he rose to leave. He stood in his sky-blue shilwar-kameez pyjama suit of baggy trousers and knee-length shirt and dirty white skull cap with a golden braid around its crest silhouetted against the sky, blue-in-blue, looking circumspectly at the mountainside. Did he want to make sure that no-one saw him leaving? Wasn't he supposed to be here? Or did he just want to be sure that no passer-by's interest in the cave was aroused? Who was to work it all out? Did I need to work it out?

By midday my thankfulness for the reed mat had almostly completely dissipated. I was so sore I didn't know how I was going to manage. I was going to have to take the chains off for at least intermittent periods in order to sit in different positions and relieve my sore spots. It was no good getting bed sores, especially as I wasn't even sick! Now would be a good time to risk taking the chains off. If the boy had been sent, it wasn't likely that anyone else would be coming soon. If he had come on his own it was likely that he knew no-one else was around. I undid the chains and stretched. It was wonderful until the searing pain in my right shoulder cut in as I tried to stretch my arms and back as well. I had grown accustomed to the dull sensation in my shoulder as the other discomfort masked it. I stayed near the chains, should anyone suddenly come. At the slightest sound I dived for the mat and slipped into the chains. It proved to be quicker than unhooking and rehooking them. The fastest way was just to wrap them around without hooking, but if anyone did come, the chances I would be found out were greater.

My thoughts were my prayers, again I was trying to follow my family's routine. Would they be sticking to the daily routine, or had everything fallen apart at the seams? I had to assume they were, had to have something to orientate my thoughts by. I needed an anchor-point to keep myself from drifting. The simple question of whether they were still in Pakistan or had been evacuated by the mission to Finland brought too much uncertainty.

I wanted to believe they were safe, harboured and consoled, encouraged. Yet I could only envision them in our own home, alone.[1] There was nothing they could do for me here, only perhaps be a source of added concern and pressure for those who were mediating – if contact had been established at all! How much money would they be demanding? Was the church dealing with them or our mission representative? Had anyone come from Finland with powers to act? I tried to fight the thoughts back, it wasn't helping my situation.

Again there was the rattle of stones rolling down the mountainside and the young man from Jamrud entered the cave with some food in a small steel bowl. It was boiled squash with a small chilli pepper. But there was a large, fresh flat whole wheat *naan*. He sat down opposite me in the haystack right where I had hidden the bread. I could see him in my mind's eye digging in the hay for the solid object that didn't belong, but he didn't move at all. The bread must have been so soft that it wasn't noticeable. If it was soft, it was probably squashed. That

[1] My family was, in fact, in our home the whole time and very well taken care of as well as consoled by local Pakistani friends and other missionaries.

was no problem as I now had more. If I only could manage to hang on to the rest of it when he took the dish back. I wouldn't be able to exchange the old bread in the haystack for this if he were sitting on it! My mind was churning, trying to work out all the details of establishing some measure of security for myself and preparing for my escape.

I ate the squash and a little of the bread, hoping to keep the rest by telling him I couldn't eat it now, wanted to eat it slowly. It was the truth, my stomach had shrunk and I felt full just from the little bit I had eaten, although I knew it was not enough to sustain me. Keeping the bread in my hand, I put the cup down. Then, nibbling at the bread I asked him if he couldn't arrange for me to bathe. He nodded knowingly and mumbled something about it being done *insha-allah*, so God will. I wondered if it was another empty promise . . .

After a while he unceremoniously got up and left. I had managed to hang on to the bread. I decided it wiser not to share it with the vermin in the haystack, so wrapped it in the chadar as extra cushioning for my pillow. It didn't matter if it got squashed – at least it would remain relatively clean! I wondered where my guard was today. Left alone I again slipped out of the chains, this time risking a look out of the mouth of the cave. Slowly I worked my way out of the mouth into the cut in front of the cave, trying to get a better view of the lie of the land on the slope where the cave was situated. Crouching low, I finally risked going all the way out to the beginning of the cut. There, hugging the hillside, I lifted my head slowly and looked back up the steep slope from behind a large clump of bunch grass growing from the edge of the cut. Not seeing anyone, I turned and studied the valley below the cave. I stayed there for several minutes, watching.

Not wanting to push my luck, I hurried back into the cave. Before long, I responded again to the urge to see what was going on outside, to get a grasp of the lie of the land. Each time I went out, I stayed for a few minutes longer. Nothing was stirring above, but as the afternoon wore on, the odd child or shepherd with a few cows or a flock of goats could be seen slowly driving the animals home across the ravine and its dried out river-bed. At first I retreated immediately upon seeing anyone, but eventually realized that as long as I was absolutely still, no-one would be able to pick me out on the mountainside, especially not in the shadow of the cut in my light grey trousers and shirt.

The track lay about fifty metres down the mountainside, but was clearly visible in the afternoon light. That was my way out. The ravine looked as if it wouldn't be passable in many places, and though the pass over the mountain across the valley was low enough, at least one flock was travelling that way, it wasn't likely to get me out of the tribal area any quicker than following the track towards civilization would.

A cascade of stones coming down the mountainside above me brought me back from my reverie with a jolt and sent me scurrying back inside the cave, my heart pounding. Had my guard seen me and come running, thinking I was going to escape? The noise increased until a she-goat jumped into the cut and three or four others crossed behind her at the opening. The large brown nanny came down the cut, turning her head slightly to get a better look into the cave. Maybe she was used to coming in to eat at the hay stored here, I thought. But how had she got in? It had been closed off with that large crate top with the Russian lettering on it. Simultaneously, I began to wonder whether a shepherd would follow her in, bringing her back to the others on their homeward course. I raised a hand to wave her off. Seeing it, she started and bolted for the open ground of the mountainside and the rest of the flock.

It took some time to recover from the scare, as harmless as it had been. By the time I ventured out into the cut again it must have been four o'clock in the afternoon. I couldn't tell the exact position of the sun from any shadows because a cloud had emerged somewhere in the west and blocked off the sun. I needed to look at the sky. The excitement of the possibility of rain made the question of time totally irrelevant. If it rained tonight, I might get a chance to escape. If they put me in the house again it would be a little more difficult, I might even have to climb the encircling wall, but if it did rain, the man would sleep inside and I would just have to escape out the door. The noise of the rain on the roof should help, even if he were to sleep in the same room. The stone wall wouldn't be a problem – not being plastered there would be plenty of hand- and footholds.

I could see it all unfolding: in the rain not even the dogs would be up and about to give warning of me leaving or approaching the settlements further down the valley. Of course I would be drenched, but what was that to freedom? Anyway, the heat was so bad, it would be almost comfortable by comparison to have the cooling effect of the rain. The only drawback would be the danger of flash floods in the lower part of the canyon. I would have to keep to high ground. With people and dogs out of the way, that shouldn't be impossible.

The prospect buoyed my spirits up. It was easier to thank God for his providence with this concrete possibility. It would, indeed, have to rain soon, the heat had held on for so many days running, there would have to be a storm soon. I was sure of it.

As dusk drew near my thoughts returned with a tinge of fear to the meeting I would be having with my captors after dark. They hadn't shown up yesterday, so they were bound to come today. They would time it as they had when they brought me here the day before yesterday: enter the valley after dark and arrive here forty-five minutes or an hour later. Would they have already been paid by someone or received promise of payment and take me somewhere else for a trade-off? I couldn't see that happening, I didn't even want to be bought free. Not only the thought of money donated for missionary work going to crooks bothered me, but the very idea of being 'bought'. I had begun to resent the idea of being tender or a commodity.

Somehow the evening came quicker than the day had gone, an anomaly I didn't comprehend. It was almost like coasting downhill. As the end of the day drew nearer the pressure seemed to lift, although the numb feeling in the pit of my stomach in apprehension of the coming meeting was still there. I would have to be aggressive in dealing with them again, warn them, banter with them. I dare not look weak or depressed. I could start by asking where the charpai they had promised was, and the proper tea 'with milk', 'the walks in the hills' the man had alluded to. I didn't have any real card to play, I would have to use whatever I had. 'Lord, help me in the confrontation too!', I prayed.

Tuesday, 8.30 p.m.

The sun had set an hour ago. Dusk had gone with no sign of anyone coming. Yesterday the man who was keeping me had come before it was completely dark. Wasn't he coming at all tonight? Would I be left alone? This might be my chance! It was now dark enough to make a break for it. If I wrapped the chadar around my shoulders, no-one more than a few yards away would recognize that I was wearing European dress. Only the legs of my trousers beneath the knee would be seen. People might be moving about yet though, both an advantage and disadvantage: I might be seen, but with people still moving about, a man walking back into town wouldn't raise any suspicion. The excitement and fear gnawed at the pit of my stomach. Should I make a break for it now or should I wait for the rain I had been hoping for? Who was to know when it might rain next? My family must be desperate, every minute that I could shorten their ordeal would spare an eternity of waiting for them. This had to be it.

Just as I was finishing the weighty deliberations and the scales were tipping in favour of making a break for it, the now familiar clatter of rolling stones above the cave changed it all. Someone was coming. I was flooded simultaneously by feelings of distress and relief: distress because I had missed the chance, relief because I had not been caught just as I was trying to escape. Why did it have to happen like this just as the coast appeared clear? I decided that any attempt at escape would have to be better prepared, not based on any spontaneous situation.

Was it my kidnappers who were coming? Would I hear now what the negotiations had resulted in? If the gangsters had called the church school number I had given them on Sunday, there would have to be some kind of decision by now. On the other hand, would the mission ask for proof I was alive before making any payment? Would there be any payment?

Captivity

They needed to refuse out of principle to protect other missionaries from becoming targets. The quandary I and the whole mission were in seemed unresolvable, a true aporia (difficulty). There seemed no way out. What was the right thing to do, protect a life or a principle? Pakistanis never had any problems in choosing between the two: the person was always more important than the issue. Was there really any conflict between the two? Why was there no simple solution? As with most true-to-life problems, there was no pat answer. A case could be made for paying, equally well a case could be made for refusing ransom. I didn't want them to pay, but I wanted to be freed. Maybe I wasn't going to get to escape after all.

Anyway, the decision to pay or not to pay would not be mine. Perhaps the ransom had already been paid and if I were to escape and be caught by someone else, it would have been wasted! Perhaps the gang was coming now to get proof that I was alive and well as a prerequisite to finalizing a deal, a letter in my own hand, dated, or a picture of me with the day's newspaper. How good it would be to have a newspaper or something else to read! Anything to concentrate my thoughts.

These thoughts flashed through my mind as the dim light from an approaching lantern cast a shadow on the cut leading into the cave. It was my guard, but there was no-one with him. Motioning me to follow, he began to lead me back up the mountainside to the house.

'Where are the other men?' I couldn't hold back, had to ask about the meeting with my captors that was two days overdue.

'I am going into town to find out tomorrow,' he replied in a mix of Pushto and broken Urdu. Apparently he was as worried as I was. If I had heard right that first night, they had promised him 400 rupees, less than £10, for looking after me. As far as I knew, however, they hadn't given him any money when they handed me over to him. Maybe he was worried that he wouldn't get paid for the risk he was taking. Four hundred rupees isn't much money even for a poor Pathan farmer; they must have told him they would be coming for me soon. What had happened?

The man motioned for me to wrap the chadar around me. Strange, too, that he was carrying a light, whereas normally he was very secretive about taking me to the house. It somehow didn't add up. Tonight there were lanterns burning in the courtyard and on the women's side of the house. I was surprised to see the young fellow from Jamrud indoors after dark. He must have been a relative of my guard's wife: the door to the women's quarters was ajar and he had obviously just come from there. No Pathan would leave any other man than immediate kin alone in his house with the womenfolk. But where had the man been last night . . . ? I hadn't seen him here then.

We were standing in the courtyard in front of the same room I had occupied the night before, but now in the light of the lantern I could see it better.

'Sit!' He used the one invective he had mastered in Urdu pointing into the room at the string bed. Someone was standing in the shadows with the grass basket that had my food on it and he was turning to have it given to me when I sat down. It must have been a child. I was preoccupied with my burning need to wash. It bordered on the rude, but I argued that it was also culturally acceptable to make full use of my status as *mehman* or 'guest' since he was after all feeding me, and I had been told I would have everything I needed. So I spoke up:

'I want to bathe before eating!' My guard looked uncomprehending. Was it the language or the thought that he couldn't grasp? He himself hadn't changed clothes since I saw him first on Sunday evening. Maybe he wasn't in the habit of bathing. Rural Pathans sometimes look as though they are not, but Pakistanis normally bathe twice a day, morning and evening. The young man intervened in Pushto, breaking the embarrassed tension. They exchanged words and finally the man told him to get water, sending the child with the food away at the same time. The young man was back presently with a bucket of water and, to my astonishment, a bar of real deodorant soap in a plastic soap box and still in its red and white paper wrapper. Where had he got 'Cusson's Imperial Leather' in a place like this? Were the women more civilized or was it his own, brought up from the city?

As he put the bucket down, I eyed the room, trying to find a place

Captivity

to stand on the dirt floor that wouldn't turn to mud once I started bathing. There were the charpais piled up along the far wall on an elevated area. That was earthen too, so it wouldn't have been any better place to stand in the water I would be pouring over me. There were farming implements and plain junk piled up along the wall in front of me. A pair of oversized paratrooper's jump-boots caught my attention. Maybe my guard wore them in the winter snows up here on the mountain. He would be able to wear any number of socks with them – if he had any . . .

The young man obviously read my thoughts as my eyes darted around the room, a tribute to his relative sophistication, for he began pulling burnt bricks out of the rubble and made a small platform of them for me to stand on while taking my bucket shower. I thanked him sincerely and began to undress, giving him ample time to leave according to the local dictates of modesty.

Before I had started my bath, he was calling from outside. I quickly dumped the bread out of the chadar before wrapping it around me to be presentable. I hid the bread in my pile of clothes, which appeared much dirtier now that I looked at them from the outside. They looked horrible with the caked dirt and sweat on the back of both shirt and trousers, the white lines where the sweat had dried repeatedly leaving a faint tinge of salt, the frayed collar and cuffs. When I stepped to the door open now to the courtyard, he was holding something out to me. My heart skipped a beat – it was hard to tell in the dark, but it looked like a shilwar-kameez suit! Taking it into the light I was exuberant. It not only was local dress, but dark grey, perfect for moving about unseen at night, and it was clean – wrinkled, but clean – still smelling of soap! I was profuse in my thanks. Then, realizing that I may have given away my intention of escaping by being overjoyed at having a costume that would let me blend in with the surroundings in every way, I tried to cover my tracks, making a point of explaining how much more comfortable the wide cut local clothing is than trousers and shirt. That was true especially when sitting in eastern fashion legs akimbo. The waist is comprised of four yards of cloth gathered by a soft cotton string.

Escape from terror

It was with undivided concentration that I dedicated my energies to getting clean. The pure animal joy at being at one with my own body again, ridding it of the grime and sweat, feeling the release of my body from the bonds of captivating and oppressing filth was almost akin to an expurgation of the soul. The wholeness of man, the unity of body and soul was an experiential reality. After all, *anima* means 'spirit'. It was like being born again as the rivulets and droplets washed away the indignity, remaining for a moment on the powder surface of the dirt floor before, as if by magic, being absorbed suddenly, turning the floor to mud. I rationed the water jealously so as to be able to lather several times, each time shedding a skin of inhibition, denigration, oppression, despicability.

Strange, how so many small things add up to create a captive's psyche. Beat a person to subdue him. Blindfold him to close him off from his surroundings. Deny him basic cleanliness and sanitation. Don't let him shave to rob him of his dignity. Hold him incommunicado to emphasize his feelings of helplessness. Tie him or chain him to destroy his spirit. Make him sit or lie on the floor, preferably in the dirt, to make him lose his self-respect. Keep changing the daily routine to enhance his feelings of insecurity. With time, he is bound to grovel, unless he has something to carry him, to support him.

I had my faith, my firm belief that God's hand was not withdrawn from me, but holding me even in this situation. One by one he had helped me to cope with each of these situations, kept my spirit up, helped me to do my utmost to change – or accept each condition. I had not cowered or expressed fear when they beat me. I had been too surprised. Maybe the shock of the situation had protected me from feeling the pain. It wasn't until afterwards that I had felt it, as now, while bathing, needing to use my right arm. I was happy that they hadn't had the satisfaction of seeing me bow to their brutality. They hadn't attempted to make use of such tactics later. Even blindfolding me had helped me to concentrate on the one who is unseen and still present, caring for and protecting me as the good shepherd. Although I was unable to see where they were taking me, I knew that he was leading me. Now having the chance to bathe, like having the lota and shovel in the cave, bolstered my self-respect, and determination to stay on top of the situation, no matter how long it lasted, no matter what happened.

How fortunate it was that I had already started to grow a beard a week before the kidnapping. Now I was glad for the camouflage. With every passing day I would look more like a hillsman. Since I had already decided to regrow my beard, I would have been feeling grubby anyway! Strange, what silly thoughts like that could do in the way of comfort . . .

Being held incommunicado meant talking more to God and listening to his consolation and guidance, depending more on his help. Being able to get out of my chains had given me feelings of freedom and almost superiority in a secretive sort of way, anything but a broken spirit. And having to sit on the bare earth turned out to be the first issue I had been able to press to my advantage with my captors. Now bathing had followed suit. I felt that I could indeed exert some influence and, with God's help, make it through this ordeal. The lack of any established routine was disconcerting, but that, too, made me rely on God minute by minute, always ready for a change of place that might bring the loss of the amenities such as I had in the cave.

I had used the last of the water. I was clean, inside and out. A long step got me from the little platform of bricks to the string bed without having to step in the mud. The shilwar-kameez soaked up the droplets off my wet skin as only old, threadbare cotton can. Pulling on the knee-length shirt I noticed that it had seen better days: the seam on the right side was open almost to the armpit. The left armpit was torn open. It didn't matter, the loose-fitting clean clothes were comfortable to the point of enjoyment.

I slipped into my shoes and presented myself at the door for scrutiny, feeling somehow silly, almost like a woman showing off her new dress, but the approval in the eyes of my guard was obvious. He even decided he'd better take the credit for this great idea, pointing out that it was his shilwar-kameez I was wearing. Why should he be happy that I looked like a hill-billy Pathan? He was concerned that no-one recognize me as a foreigner when he took me to and from the cave, should we be seen on the way. This gave him added security in the form of cover he had not thought about himself.

He called out for the food to be brought again and I sat down to my meal of bread and boiled potatoes, with the difference that I could see the contents of my bowl in the light of the lantern tonight. While no-one was looking, I exchanged the old piece of flat bread I had hidden in my clothes for a fresh one, thinking I may as well have the best of what was available. I ate with more relish feeling better after my bath, but found I still couldn't eat much. I called for the man and gave him the basket.

'Eat much bread!' he exhorted me again.

'I ate lots, plenty, thank you!'

'Sit!' he commanded, indicating the opposite end of the bed, meaning for me to turn around and stretch out my feet to the other end, which traditionally has only warp, no weave, so that the part of the bed bearing the body weight can be tightened periodically by pulling the slack out of the warp. I had been eating at the head-end of the bed, as is culturally acceptable. He handed the basket out through the door and pulled the chains out of nowhere, almost as if out of a black hat. I was disappointed, I thought that things had changed. He obviously hadn't! With the wide legs of my shilwar it wasn't any easier for him to get the chains right than it had been before. Again I felt this was an intelligence test he was failing. I decided to help him out and pulled up the leg of my shilwar as I laid my calf along the top of the side pole, making sure it was not directly on top to ensure a loose fit. That solved his problem and his fumbling came to fruition. Embarrassed, he quickly put out the light and left, closing the door behind him.

Slipping out of the chains I lay back and took stock, reminding myself not to fall asleep without them. It had been three whole days and two nights now. What had happened so far on the outside? The same thoughts always came back – how could they not as there had been no answers. If only my family could find the strength they needed to hold up. As so many times already that day I committed them, and myself, to God's merciful hands. The stage seemed set for my escape, all I needed now was the right opportunity. It was bound to come. The chains were no problem and I had local clothing. There had been that cloud in the afternoon. Perhaps the rains would come tonight and I would have a chance. I felt the adrenalin seep into my blood. Things were working out! The excitement was intense, but not enough to fight off the sleep that weighed down on me. I decided I'd better sleep now in case it did rain later. Anyway, I had my doubts. The cloud had not been visible any more against the stars when we came up from the cave . . . Back in the chains, sleep came quickly.

Wednesday 12th September, morning

Today was more of the same. I was beginning to sense the routine and finding no little consolation in it. The simple feeling that I knew what to expect took away half the stress that came from plain uncertainty.

Getting up before dawn and coming down the track from the house without any detours confirmed my idea of the lie of the land. The house was the first of two, perhaps three, built at the end of a ridge where it dropped off steeply to the south in the direction of Jamrud and Peshawar. It was separated from the higher mountains on both sides by deep ravines. It seemed that the only approach to the cluster of stone and mud dwellings was from the north along the ridge we always seemed to traverse on one end or the other. Yesterday we had come down the western side of the ridge to cross over at the northern end. When I got the chance to run for it, I would have to start out up the ridge and then double back down into the gully, where I had heard the sound of rushing water. With water there would be vegetation and therefore cover.

I wondered why the track was on the opposite side of the ridge, away from the water, where normally one would expect to find settlements, agriculture and the traffic presenting the need for a thoroughfare. The need would simply create it in the time-worn fashion of animals and humans the world over by wearing a track into the face of the earth where it offered the least resistance. Anyway, it was good for me that the traffic would be far out of sight and ear-shot. It felt good to make plans, keeping my mind alert and my hopes up.

Being alone in the cave with my thoughts and my Maker was an intensely spiritual experience, regardless, or perhaps because of, the sheer physicality of my confinement. Especially the mornings between 4 a.m. and about noon, when tea would be likely to come, were a time of soul searching. There were no interruptions, no visitors, I had lots of opportunity to reflect on the shallowness of my life. Shallowness is an inherently relative term, and is perhaps relative to the point of irrelevance when compared from the outside, but experiencing it in the fibre of my person, it was absolute. It is one thing to be ignorant of one's superficiality, another to ignore it. I guessed that shallowness bothered those the least, who had no depth at all. I wondered if this was why I was here. Did I need to be shaken this hard in order to recognize and accept the challenges before me?

Of course the thoughts I was having were thoughts I had brought with me seminally. I was made particularly conscious of the fact that only complete dedication can bring about the kind of change that is needed in our world. Throughout history it had been people with a singleness of purpose and an unflinching commitment whom God had used to cause change. How many loyalties and so-called priorities did I have? What did it have to say about the effectiveness of my ministry? Would I ever be able to concentrate on the essential, if I made it out of here? If . . .

The question nagged and haunted me. What was essential in my life? At times I felt guilty that I had not concentrated more on deep theological study, not exercised discipline over the space and time I had been given to live in. The monograph I had started work on several years before lay dormant on magnetic diskettes, unattended to for four years now, even though I felt it to be an enormously important topic with widespread ecumenical ramifications. On the other hand, I would have felt even more guilty if I had shirked my responsibilities as a father and husband for the sake of finishing a book. I had come to feel that making the Christian faith apply to the intricacies and unavoidabilities of daily life in the family was more important than getting it right on paper. It certainly was no easier for us in our inter-cultural marriage and with our personalities than for anyone else.

Still, the dream had followed me constantly, alternately thirsting for fulfilment and poisoning my mind with the bile of feelings of guilt, inadequacy and helplessness at not being able to accomplish what I wanted with the time, energy and responsibilities I had.

Beyond the gnawing knowledge of my inadequacies was the constant certainty of God's grace and love for me, his protection and care. 'Thy rod and thy staff, they comfort me . . .'

After reconstructing the twenty-third psalm in my memory on Monday from the various languages I had learned it in so many years previously, I had been contemplating it, in a way living off it. Other portions of scripture had come back as well, particularly ones I had been through with the new bishop at his preparatory retreat on Friday and Saturday.

At his request we had read St Paul's letters to Timothy. That had made sense because it gave instructions on how to choose a bishop. Not that there was any choice in the matter now, but they did recount what a bishop should be like. Strange that the letters had also contained a reference to kidnappers, 'menstealers', grouped together with 'whoremongers, manslayers, murderers of fathers and mothers' and all sorts of other 'nice' people who, as 'lawless, disobedient, ungodly, profane and unholy sinners' needed the law.

The people here in the semi-autonomous tribal areas surely needed the law, that was for sure. That was precisely what had been bothering me about the Islamic Republic of Pakistan for a long time already, albeit in an unarticulated, partially subconscious way. Didn't they have it, the law, in Islam? They had it in the Qur'an, in the Sunnat, in the Hadith, in the Shariat. Why, then, didn't it have the desired effect? Much of it, if not most of it, was compatible with or derived from Mosaic law. Then again, the law had never yet produced life, that was the province of the Spirit. 'The letter killeth . . .'

There were so many topics of acute relevance to our situation, to the bishop in his new-found calling as well as things that spoke to me in my life setting: 'Let no man despise your youth, be rather an example of the believers in speech, actions, in Christian love, in Spirit, in faith, in purity . . . Attend to reading, teaching, doctrine. Do not neglect the gift that is in you . . . Concentrate on these things, give yourself completely to them . . . (1 Timothy 4:12-15). Was that where the questions plaguing me now, here in the cave, had come from?

Could it be that it had only been last week, four days ago? Since then eternities had passed. Peshawar, the bishop, my work, it was all light years away. I remembered how shocked I had been when the moderator of the Church of Pakistan asked me to arrange the two day time of prayer, Bible-study and fasting for the new bishop. I was to accompany him through the time of inner preparation for his new form of ministry as a bishop in the Church of Pakistan. I wondered how my colleagues had felt about it. I had the strange feeling that some thought I was 'sucking up to the locals' or trying to look important. Just because people are missionaries doesn't mean they can't have base thoughts.

How could I serve as confessor and mentor to someone whom I would be working under immediately afterwards? How would he react to it? On the other hand I was grateful that the moderator had enough faith in me to ask me to do his job. Now I realized that I had needed the time of meditation and preparation. It had been necessary to prepare me for this experience, perhaps more acutely than the new bishop. Sitting alone or together with the new bishop in the ancient Moghul tomb that had been converted first into headquarters for the Frontier Corps in the early days of the British occupation of Peshawar and later into a chapel, I had gathered inner strength for this ordeal.

During the interim without a local bishop I had been so busy keeping the Diocese afloat that I had lost scope and sense of proportion as to what was really important. Falling into the duties of treasurer head first, I had been taken by surprise. On just a few days' notice I had had to take over all the responsibilities relating to the finances of the church in the whole province. Ill prepared for the job as I was, I had had to work over-time. I hadn't had the time to look after my own well-being, physically or spiritually. I was tired, tense, nervous. There had been problems at home that had developed over a long period of time, problems that had become chronic, problems that had given me a peptic ulcer already during our second year in Pakistan. Had I fled the situation into work, tried to find relief and recognition in succeeding at least in my job?

Those two days of prayer and fasting had been time well spent. How would I have managed here without them? I wondered . . .

I was concerned with the basics here. Survival. I repeatedly thanked God for the shovel and the spouted lota water-pot. It made maintaining a semblance of hygiene and keeping the cave free of flies and stench so much easier.

The guard hadn't come yet today. No, he was in town trying to find out why no-one had shown up yet. What time would he be back with news? After bearing responsibility for me for three nights, he was getting nervous, probably wanting to know what was happening as badly as I did.

It was hard to believe this was the fourth day already. On the one hand days were so long, time stood still. On the other hand, looking back, the time had passed quickly. The incongruity lay in the fact that while the last four days had gone by speedily, the time before that was dark and dim history. An age had transpired. Completely cut off from my normal life, life had begun in a new time and new place. Everything else seemed utterly remote and from an age so long ago that it was already unreal.

Did Marja-Liisa know by now what had happened? The question wouldn't leave me, no matter how often I asked it of myself. I had no answer to it. Was she coping under the strain? Did she and the others in Peshawar know more about my fate by this time than I did? Had they been negotiating or even settled a ransom? That possibility set me on edge. I could be free and back home by tonight if the man were to bring the news with him that a settlement had been reached. That possibility was mind-boggling. Could freedom be so close as to be attainable today? What if they had paid, but he didn't find out? What if I were to escape when I had already been ransomed, but didn't know? Even if I made it, the ransom would have been wasted. And if someone else in tribal territory picked me up, they might have to pay a second ransom! It seemed a no-win situation. It was so confusing it felt better not to think about it for as long as possible . . . In the end it seemed that the longer it took for me to try an escape, the greater the possibility would be that money had already changed hands. I needed a chance soon!

At mid-morning the redhead brought me *sayviyyan*, sweet spaghetti cooked in milk. That was something people ate only on festive occasions. Instead of the dented and bent tin cup I usually got my food in, it was served in a pretty porcelain bowl with black and gilt trim, imported Japanese ware. Marja-Liisa and I had looked at the same dinner service in the smugglers' bazaar when we came to Pakistan in February 1986. We might have bought it if we had not wanted something plain and less remarkable, more suited to our position as missionaries.

What did it mean? I pondered the puzzle it presented me as I enjoyed the change of diet and utensils. Compared with what I had been getting it was rich food and I was full after just a few mouthfuls. It was almost torture to continue eating as the boy looked on after I had finished only half the plate. Then it came to me suddenly: the man was in town today. Did the effort at feeding me signal that the rest of the household sympathized with me? It was an encouraging thought. Was it something that could be built on? I forced myself to eat the whole plate, feeding myself slowly with my fingers, there being no cutlery. A feeling of satisfaction was growing in me: were things beginning to fall into place for my escape? On a meal like this I could walk a good distance. Would the family of my guard help me to escape?

The new hopes and possibilities kept my thoughts going. But a clean body, fresh clothes and a full stomach proved to be a good sedative as well. Stretching out diagonally on the mat that had been left in the cave I extended it with my shoes and, on top of them, the bread wrapped in the chadar for a pillow. I was able to shorten the day with sleep.

In the late afternoon the man returned, carrying his kalashnikov again and looking worried, the thin, dark features drooping in a bothered frown and his whole, slight body stooped under an invisible load.

Captivity

He brought me a bowl of rice, hidden under the chadar draped over his arm. He squatted, poured himself a cup of water from the lota and placed the rice in front of me, admonishing me to eat. He didn't have the cotton wool in his ear anymore, so it wasn't likely that it was his earache that was bothering him.

'Aadmi margiya!' Again this talk of a man getting killed. It didn't sound like a warning to me not to try to escape in this area he loved to call 'Ajjilabad'. This time someone had died, that was why he was carrying the gun, I speculated. He was probably expecting tribal war to break out over the killing.

Every year the press reported some widespread bloody feud involving whole villages being fought out in tribal territory. Recently there had been a miniature war between Shia and Sunni clans in this area, a couple of valleys to the south-west. In the last few years they had started using grenade launchers and rockets besides machine guns and the standard assault rifles, by-products of the ongoing conflict across the border in Afghanistan. Studying the man, my thoughts began to change. This wasn't a tribal conflict, a Pathan doesn't worry about that kind of thing where one's honour is at stake. On the contrary, he revels in the chance to gain glory in battle and to establish his honour. This problem concerned him personally and had to do with me. The silent knowledge hit home hard. The contentment and hopes I had harboured since receiving the sayviyyan were supplanted by the gnawing knowledge, more in the pit of my stomach than in my conscious thoughts, that one of the gang members had been killed. Why was he confiding in me? I needed to confirm my gut feeling:

'It was one of my kidnappers?' He nodded dejectedly and got up to leave.

'Did it happen today?' I queried, my stomach forming a knot.

'Yesterday.' Of course, it would have taken time for the news to travel, even if word of mouth in the sub-continent always has been the most efficient, and often most accurate, form of information, the media being full of non-news or disinformation.

I had hardly touched the rice. It was awful, although I was sure that he had meant it to please me. Maybe he had cooked it himself: it was a gooey mess with no salt. It couldn't have been made by the same person who had prepared the sayviyyan. He obviously didn't know that I had already had something to eat and wouldn't understand that I wasn't hungry at all. Again I forced myself to eat, but it was harder still than trying to finish the sayviyyan. While he stood immersed in thought at the mouth of the cave with his back to me, I managed to force a quarter of the goo down. I hastily compacted the remainder onto one side of the dish, making it look as if I had eaten more than half. When he turned, I offered it back to him protesting that my stomach had shrunk, not an untruth, though not 'the whole truth and nothing but the truth'. He remonstrated with me, encouraging me to eat it all. In his state of dejection he didn't have the determination to override my protests, so he took the bowl and left, flinging the contents down the hill.

He left me with my thoughts spinning dizzily. One of the men had been killed. What would be the outcome? I realized I should have been afraid of revenge, but somehow couldn't help feeling a sort of relief, not at the death itself, more because at least something had happened, even if it was awful. The stagnation had ended with that knowledge. Things were being brought into motion, as long as things were happening, something good might happen. Instead of fearing repercussions or reciprocation I felt strangely secure. Perhaps his bringing the rice had done it – and the fact that he had shown no anger, only despondency. Who had told him? And what had they told him? How was this development being interpreted? Most important of all, what had really happened?

It didn't take long for the fellow from Jamrud to come. Should I discuss it with him, would he know?

'I hear one of the men got killed.' I decided to give it a go. He was not only willing, but anxious to talk.

'Two. It was God's work, they were caught by chance.' Behind the mask of Muslim stoicism in the face of fate I thought I detected both fear and sorrow. He probably was related, as I had suspected from the start. He recounted the story:

'They had rented a "Daksun" and were caught at a road-block in Barra Agency'. He reiterated the story in some detail. Did he have it from my guard, or did he have his own sources? Where things were unclear, I questioned him and he answered readily enough. Two or three of the men – he wasn't sure whether the driver of the pickup was one of the gang or not – were entering the area around Barra, a smuggler's haven to the south-west of Peshawar on the border of the North West Frontier Province. As a part of the Tribal Territories it was not under the full jurisdiction of the Islamic Republic of Pakistan. When they came upon a road-block manned by *Khasadaars*, the paramilitary force maintained by the government's Political Agent in the Tribal Territories, there had been trouble. The 'PA' was a relic from British colonial rule, like so much of the judiciary, executive and military in the subcontinent.

Road-blocks are common in the Tribal Area, one of the few ways to maintain a semblance of control. Although, theoretically, there to seal off a given area hermetically, in practice they are only intimidating spot checkpoints, especially in the heat of the day, when the people manning them try to stay in the shade of a nearby tree or lean-to. The men had tried to do what most innocent travellers try to get away with, bluff their way through without stopping, just as they had done when they were smuggling me out of Peshawar on Sunday. It was usually a test of wills. The driver slowed to establish that he recognized the checkpoint and to avoid bottoming out on the speed-breaker if the boom was up. If it was down, he would keep inching toward it in an effort to will the junior sepoy manning it to raise it without any search or checking of documents. The sepoy, in turn, watched the literate sub-constable standing on the roadside, ready to check papers and make a search of the vehicle. If the car got past the sub-constable without him hollering, up went the boom. If it was already up and the driver got past the officer and could see in his rear view mirror that he had turned his back, waiting for the next vehicle, he accelerated past the checkpoint, knowing full well that the boom wouldn't be lowered without the junior officer's order. Some of the cooler customers tried to drive through without taking any notice of the police, and often got away with it, as there are usually no chase vehicles or radio connections at the checkpoints. Even more important and inhibiting to the forces manning the checkpoints was their constant fear that they might inconvenience a big shot by forcing him to stop. That could cost them their job and more. So small fry played on that knowledge also. In Pakistan, a powerful man might be dressed like a dumpy peasant; how was an uneducated policeman to know Who's Who? No-one would dare to think of shooting the tyres out on a car he wasn't certain did not belong to any influential person.

As chance would have it, at this road-block a khasadaar recognized a face. He was sure it belonged to the 'Phantom', a criminal they had been on the alert for more than six months now, wanted on charges of murder, robbery, theft, abduction, rape . . . So when the pickup didn't stop in spite of his challenge, he shot out the tyres and they dragged the men from the car.

Where the young man got his facts I'll never know, but he was confident in reporting that the two men had been shot in cold blood after the following 'interrogation':

'What are you doing in Barra?' the khasadaar demanded.

'Nothing! We're just visiting friends,' the kidnappers protested.

'You're lying! Wherever you go you make mischief!' Was the final verdict implemented with shots to the heart from point-blank range?

It was one of those things that sounded like a cover-up designed to reap sympathy for his wronged relatives, who were really not such bad people as one thought. Innocents being executed on the spot without a trial . . . It sounded concocted for a purpose, yet I could see it happening. If the police in the cities handed out guns to men to kill their wives for adultery, simply taking the men's word for it, what would hinder them in non-incorporated areas like this from taking the law into their own hands.[2]

[2]The official version that came out in the press that day complete with group photo and mug shots of the deceased, of which I had, of course, no knowledge at that time, was that there had been a shoot-out of an 'Islamic lashkar of their own tribe', an 'Islamic host', had wreaked vengeance on these 'bad elements' of their society. It was 'an internal affair of the tribe'. The whole official version was so obviously 'smoke', that I am sometimes inclined to believe that the dacoits' version is closer to the truth. As I was to learn from various police sources themselves in the course of time, the disinformation was designed to protect the authorities from the wrath of the tribesmen.

Captivity

All I knew at this point was that the two had been shot by the authorities. Did it have anything to do with me? Were the police on to them? Had it really been 'chance', like the man had said? I knew that from my point of view it had not been chance. From the very start I had been convinced, and had tried to convince the gang, that God was taking care of me. Hadn't I told the one with no beard that if they wanted to try and barter with God they would have to take the consequences? I hadn't meant it as a threat, but as a fact. God will not be mocked. It was difficult for me to grasp the possible repercussions of the event, but I felt that things would be better for me now, not worse, although revenge would have been the normal outcome.[3]

Later the guard came back with tea. He was being more hospitable since he came back from town, first the rice and now five o'clock tea.

'No enemy, you, me!' He was trying to tell me that there was no enmity between us, that he had no personal interest in keeping me, let alone harming me: it was the others' fault, he wasn't one of them.

He probably wasn't. If I had heard right that first night and they had only promised him 400 rupees, then his major fault was stupidity.

I nodded my agreement, but wanted to qualify it.

'You have no reason to keep me, you should let me go!'

The confused look on his face told it all. He didn't want to keep me, it was getting too dangerous for his taste. On the other hand he was afraid of letting me go too. He had his own *majboori*, the patent excuse for people in these parts: he wasn't free to do as he wanted, he, like 120 million of his compatriots on a normal day, was shirking the individual responsibility that he had before God and man by pleading 'obligations'. No-one dared question a *majboori*, the whole net of social inter-relationships would fall apart if that were to happen. The system of *layn-dayn*, the very fibre of society's infrastructure, was a

[3]The Deputy Inspector General of Police told me later that there was an unwritten understanding between them and kidnappers: The police would not raid the dacoits or attempt any armed intervention if the criminals would not harm their prisoners. Judging by what I had experienced I felt that he had probably only been trying to convince me after-the-fact that I had not been in any real danger. Obviously the equilibrium between the authorities and the criminal elements was not very stable.

relationship of give and take based on reciprocal obligations stemming from favours or support granted.

There was a cheap version of *majboori* too. The men who had nabbed me, claimed they were forced to do it 'because their children were starving and the power brokers of society were sucking the blood of the poor'. Our modern-day Robin Hood. Cheap cop-outs all of it. Despicable spinelessness, shirking the basic responsibility of every human being to provide for himself and his family by the sweat of his brow. They had paid for it in the only accepted currency, with their lives. 'He who lives by the sword shall die by the sword' was a phrase that came often to mind since I learned the news.

'I heard that there were two killed . . .' I dropped it as a question to see whether the two men had the same source and to try to confirm this newer information.

'Yes, two,' he frowned, a sorry sight.

'The two leaders? The bearded one who drove and the clean-shaven one who handed me over to you?' My own words cut me to the quick. Had I said too much letting him know that I could identify the men?

'The bearded one and the clean-shaven one!' He confirmed, looking up in surprise at me. How could I know? I was surprised myself at having put my finger on the right ones intuitively. I had somehow been sure. It was a gut feeling. Was that what inspiration is like, a gut feeling? After all, by now there were at least ten of the gang involved: the five who had abducted me, then two who replaced the men who had jumped out of the car on the way to the first village, the *dalaal* acting as an intermediary, the 'big gun' who had refused to take me off their hands, the young fellow who had shown them the way to this hide-out, probably the brother of the young fellow I suspected to be the brother-in-law of my guard. Getting it right the first time was a chance of one in a hundred!

'Listen!' I said, trying to make the most of the spell I had unwittingly cast, 'the two were killed on Tuesday, two days after I was kidnapped. There were five of them, two are already gone. God forbid that any more should die. You'd better let me go!' Somehow in

he situation it didn't seem overblown at all to insinuate that the men
vere getting killed at the rate of one a day, as outrageous as it appears
ven to me now.

He nodded his full agreement once again, but couldn't bring
imself to make a commitment. Instead he said someone would surely
e coming today. Everything would sort itself out.

'You and I both know that these guys were *badmaashes*. They were
oodlums and got what they deserved. No-one needs to cry for them!
ut just think of the suffering their wives and children will go through
ow that they are dead and no longer there to provide for them.' I tried
o imagine the wives beating their breasts, tearing at their hair,
lternately crying in shrill shrieks of pain and groaning in animal
gony, swaying to and fro seated amidst the other women of the tribe,
heir dirty and dishevelled children wiping their runny noses and tear-
ained cheeks on the shoulders of big sisters and grandmothers, afraid to
ee their mothers so demented. Would they have a *shamiana*, an awning,
o sit under out of the heat of the glaring sun and in a spot open enough
o accommodate the tens of women who would come to weep and wail
vith them? Or would they be alone, outcast dependants of criminal
lements? Would their husbands even receive a proper Islamic burial? I
ouldn't guess. I truly felt sorry for the women. What fault of theirs was
t that the men were criminals? They would have to bear the penalty of
esolation and poverty their men had earned for them. Their grief was
orn of fear and an utter sense of helplessness and insecurity. At least in
heir cases the hopelessness of their wailing would be real; they
vouldn't need professional 'wailing women'. Only two options were
vailable to them, neither very enticing: life as beggars or harlots.

A thought was forming in my mind. Normally, Muslims pray *fateha*,
Surah of the Qur'an for the 'departed souls' of their deceased. As a
Christian, I believed that prayer for the living is needed. Why not pray
or the wives and children?

'It's no use praying for the dead men anymore, and to tell the truth,
don't feel any sorrow for them. They got what they had coming. But
vhat have the widows and orphans done to deserve such worthless
usbands who lived a life that got them killed? Who is going to

provide for their families now? Let's pray for their families,'
suggested. He gaped at me in utter consternation, unable to fathom
why I would want to pray for them, the relatives of my adversaries. He
cupped his hands upward on his knees in the Islamic position for
supplicatory prayer as he sat cross-legged on the earthen floor of the
cave. Maybe he complied simply for lack of an answer.

'Almighty God, giver – and taker – of life, you alone hold the secret
of life and death in your almighty hand. You have seen the deeds of
the men whose lives you have required. It is yours to judge. For their
wives and children we pray. You know the needs they will face, the
loneliness they will have to cope with, the difficulties they will have,
the grief they will bear. Don't let them suffer for the evils of the
deceased. Allow them to see the light of your truth, that the darkness
of their lives might be dispelled. And Lord, we pray for this people
caught in its lawlessness and fear, that it might recognize your holy will
and live according to it. Amen.'

I raised my head to find him in a daze, perhaps silently praying his
own prayer, cut off from the world around him. Suddenly he came to
with a start and bolted from his sitting posture of prayer, like a child
who had been caught doing some thing he shouldn't.

When had he prayed last? Muslims must pray five times a day, but
even whose who don't often pause for prayer when they pass the shrine
of a *Piir*, the grave of a locally revered 'saint'. Childless women, men in
financial difficulty, people who need something they feel God might
give them, if only the Piir would intercede on their behalf. It was
something that had always bothered me and it wasn't even in keeping
with the strict monotheism in the orthodox Islam of the Qur'an,
Sunnah and Hadith, which accepts no mediator between God and
man. Not even Christ, who is described as such in the Bible they claim
to accept as one of the 'Four Books': the Law, the Psalms, the Gospel
and the 'Repetition' or Qur'an. In practice, however, God is
envisioned as so far away, so distant and detached, that he could not
possibly take an interest in a normal individual's life or hear one's
prayers without the *shifaarish* or representation of someone closer to
God than the petitioner himself. Folk Islam operates on the tenet that

Captivity

Muhammad is the prime mediator and holy men can serve that function as well, whether alive or departed from this life. The parallel to the veneration of saints in Christianity at the time of the spread of Islam is obvious. Whether it goes back to a basic need in unenlightened minds or to an historical dependence, or to both, I couldn't say.

My guard scurried off up the mountainside after I had finished the short and simple prayer. Perhaps the simple thought of his prisoner praying with him had been disconcerting. I remembered another time when I had prayed with a Muslim in just as unlikely a situation. I had been sitting on a low wall opposite a Piir's shrine on a mountaintop at Thandiani 2,800 m. above sea level in the foothills of the Himalaya and Karakorum mountain ranges. The Piir's shrine was really an ancient holy tree, sanctified for Islam by linking a Muslim saint to it so that the people who worshipped there would convert to Islam. A wanderer stopped to lift his hands in prayer. Scores of little rags were tied to the tree and little lanterns and bottles of oil placed among its roots as they had been from Buddhist times, 2,000 years ago in the day of Ashoka, the reformer Buddhist king, who ruled much of what is now northern India and Tibet from the valleys sprawled out at the feet of these majestic peaks. When the ragged-looking man had finished his prayer by passing his hands over his beard, an ancient practice swearing to the truth of one's words, he looked in my direction, said a word of greeting and finding that I replied, came over to talk.

I asked him why he should want to pray to a Piir instead of directly to God. He answered straightforwardly enough: 'God loved this man. He will listen to his requests!'

'Doesn't God love you?' I countered, giving an unbelieving look. He hadn't really thought of that possibility. It had never dawned on him that his Maker might be interested in him, even though he had always been interested in God, trying to fulfil his religious duty. In fact that was how he had ended up spending the last six years of his life in an insane asylum.[4] He told me his story:

[4]People dread insane asylums more than prisons in Pakistan, and not without reason, even though the prisons are dreadful places!

Escape from terror

'I was in Islamabad at the newly-constructed Faisal Mosque (the largest covered place of worship in the Muslim world) where I wanted to say my *namaaz* prayers. You have to understand that in Islam everyone is equal, anyone who is a Muslim can belong to the *jamaa'at* (congregation) for prayers. Anyone who will speak the *kalma* (creed) and has performed the *wuzu* ritual washings can join in. But when I tried to enter the mosque, police stopped me at the door. I told them I wanted to join in the prayers, but they said I couldn't, President Zia-ul-Haq had come to pray and only his entourage would be admitted. I was furious. It was against everything Islam holds holy. I tried to push my way past. After all, I had gone through the ritual washings and the time for these particular prayers would soon be over. The policemen resisted and a fight ensued. I was beside myself with rage at this breach of Islam. They beat me, overpowered me, put me in chains and took me off to a mental hospital. This is not *Pak-i-stan* (the land of the pure), it is *Zaalim-i-stan* (the land of the cruel).'

We talked on. Suddenly he surprised me by saying he wanted me to pray. Right there by the road side! The westerner in me had balked with embarrassment and theological insecurities, but the Christian in me had prevailed to pray with him, and for him, to ask God's blessing on his life, to ask that he might experience God's love for him personally through Christ.

Here in the cave the initiative had been mine, but the experience just as special. Both of us had been surprised by the idea and – at least I believed – touched by the experience.

Wednesday, evening

The sun had set at least an hour ago. Twilight had already passed, still no-one had come for me, not even to bring food. Would I have to go without food tonight? Not that I was hungry. The sayviyyan and rice-mush still lay on my stomach. Anyway, I had the bread I was saving just in case this should happen – or got a chance to escape. Escape. As at this time yesterday the obsession with the thought took over.

Captivity

Was I going to be left for the night? Alone? Perhaps this was the chance I'd been waiting for! It was dark enough now to move about without being seen, the moon would not be out for another four or five hours and I had local clothing now just the right colour to blend in with the rocky surroundings. On the other hand it might also prove difficult to find my way in total darkness. I could go now and hide somewhere down in the ravine until the moon came up, then move on.

It didn't feel right. If the guard were on his way at this very minute, he might see or hear me leaving the cave. Even if he came just a little later he would have the advantage as my head start would have been negligible, not knowing the way, only the general direction I would have to go. I would need a decent head start, leaving at a time when I could be reasonably certain that he would not miss me for a few hours. I had learned that yesterday. Just after a visit would be best: let him leave and then take off as soon as the coast was clear. That is, unless he actually wanted me to flee!

The idea came over me suddenly. Did he want to be rid of me? Especially now, after the deaths? He had been afraid today, I was sure of it. Was he more afraid of having to deal with the crooks than the khasadaars? Did he know that the chains were loose enough for me to get out of them? Had he put them on like that purposely from the beginning? I doubted it. His fumbling with them had been too real to be faked. In the end he had worked out how to hook the lock through the right links, only by now he had got used to the looseness and didn't fix them really tight, as I strained slightly against them as he hooked the lock on them. If he wanted me to escape now, after the deaths, he wouldn't have started getting the lock right.

As I debated these points in my mind I was jarred back to full alertness by a noise. As my ears strained to make out what was coming, I was hit again by a feeling of being caught in the act and the fear that went with it. I also felt the same intense sense of relief at not having left yet. Someone was coming, by the growing noise of the rolling rocks it could have been several men. There was also talking. Had the remaining gang members come? Would they be angry and eager for revenge at their collaborators' deaths? 'Lord, help me to face them, if it's them!' I breathed a prayer.

It wasn't. With relief I recognized the silhouette of my guard and the young fellow from Jamrud against the ultramarine of the starlit sky as they descended along the rim of the cut. I was surprised at the carefree way they talked. Perhaps it was because they were later tonight than normal. People would be in their homes by now, no longer moving about, unlikely to hear them talking.

My guard sent the boy back up the hill for tea and called out to him to bring a charpai. So tonight was going to be spent in the cave! Would they leave me alone here, or would the younger one be left as a guard? The older one was carrying his kalashnikov; he would be looking after me, I guessed.

He had my food with him. He opened my chains and let me stand in the mouth of the cave for a few minutes to get the kinks out, then handed me the tin dish and some bread, motioning to come out into the shallow end of the cut to eat it where there was a cool breeze. Was he being friendly now after the deaths, or was there some other motive I couldn't fathom? Why hadn't he taken me to the house? Did they have visitors? Was he himself afraid of the rest of the gang coming now under the changed circumstances.

The food proved to be a change of diet: mung beans cooked with red chilli and salt, not one of my favourites, but good for a change and rich in protein. It would stick with me for quite some time if I did get the chance to escape tonight . . .

I soon saw why he wanted me outside the cave. He went in and lit the older, smaller pile of hay in the back of the cave. In no time, smoke billowed out of the mouth of the cave and he came running out, coughing.

'What are you doing that for?' I asked, nonplussed by the unlikeliness of his behaviour.

'*Machhar* – mosquitos,' he said, with a secret smile that left me wondering what he was so pleased about. Perhaps he was congratulating himself on the idea. He certainly was being considerate for a

hange! Or was it because he was planning to stay here tonight? He
adn't thought of fumigating the place earlier . . .

I finished my meal, leaving what I couldn't eat of the small portion
n the dish and stealthily exchanging my old bread for some fresh
under the cover of darkness.

'Eat lots of bread!' he remonstrated with me again.

'I ate lots, it was too much! Thank you very much!'

We sat there in the dark, waiting for the smoke to clear in the cave.
t kept billowing in a pillar of cloud. I wondered how many people up
nd down the valley could see the white cloud against the blackness of
he night.

My guard went into the cave and came back with the reed mat. He
notioned for me to sit with him on the small flat spot in front of the
ut. We sat for a few moments in silence before the boy with the string
ed came over the crest and began his descent. The man's ten-year-
old boy followed along carrying the tea he had sent for. We got up to
ake the bed off him where he was lowering it into the cut. It seemed
o big, filling the entrance completely, its four legs barely reaching the
round with the side poles tight up against the walls of the cut.

Smoke still emitted from the cave, so we left it where it was under
he open sky halfway up the cut to the entrance of the cave. Then we
at down to wait for it to clear. The charpai was for me. I could hardly
believe it. I'd been asking for one from the very first day!

The attempt at better food, smoking out the cave, the string bed,
hey definitely were making an effort now to please me. Did it have
omething to do with the deaths? I imagined it must.

My guard had sent the young fellow and the little boy back right
way. We shared the pot of sweet black tea, the silence of the night and
he breeze descending from the mountain tops behind us. He lay a few
ards away on the reed mat swatting at the mosquitos that he had made
bereft of a home. I wasn't too bothered by them. Was it because I was
nearer the source of the smoke or was I just used to them by now?

The parable of the house purged of its demons came to mind.
Would the mosquitos bring their friends with them when they
eturned to share my abode when the smoke had cleared?

It really was a comical sight, my guard sometimes waving his chadar, sometimes swiping with his white skull cap at the swarm. All else failing, lying on his back, he would fan them off with the long shirt-tails of his *kameez* like a farmer's wife shooing the chickens away with her apron. It went on and on for the poor man and since the smoke refused to clear in the cave, we couldn't take refuge there. After an hour or so it became clear to him that it was useless waiting to get into the cave. Perhaps he also remembered that it would be stuffy in there with no breeze at all. He got up and motioned for me to put my leg on the side pole of the charpai so he could chain me up.

'The mosquitos bothering you?' I tried some small talk. He wasn't in a talking mood.

'Sidha karo!' he grunted, telling me to straighten my leg out on top of the side pole of the string bed.

'You know, it's not really necessary . . .' I tried again to get him to leave the chains off. Not because I couldn't get out of them, but for comfort's sake. Besides, I wanted to see whether he had begun to trust me or whether he had decided to make it easier for me to get away. Since he was starting to be almost nice to me, I thought it was worth a try.

'Necessary!' came the inevitable duo-syllabic reply of his pidgin Urdu. After fastening the chain, he lay back on the mat, evidently bent on getting some sleep. The mosquitos were bent on keeping him awake. He couldn't lie still for a minute. He was constantly flagellating, trying to keep them off.

I couldn't work it out. Were all the mosquitos attacking him, or had I simply got used to them? Usually if anyone got bitten I did! He was still at it when I fell asleep.

The moon had just come up when I awoke suddenly to find the man gone. By the moonlight I could see clearly that the mat was folded double and a large rock placed on it to keep it from being blown down the mountainside by the downdraughts. Excitement gripped me as with an iron hand, immobilizing me, pinning me to the charpai, sharpening my senses to a razor edge. The silence of the night turned into a cacophony of amplified minute sounds.

Captivity

My mind was churning. My guard must have had enough of the mosquitos – was he sitting further up the hill in the breeze? I sat up and craned to get a look. He wasn't close by. Carefully, I stood up on the bed and looked over the edge of the cut, careful to keep my head behind the clump of bunch grass growing precariously in the loose sand and rocks on the edge. Gingerly my eyes tested the slope, making a long, slow sweep from the mat down and out across the mountainside, searching out the boulders to see if any of them moved. Craning my neck I looked around the clump of grass up the ascent towards the house hiding in the darkness of the distance. He was nowhere visible in the bright moonlight swathing the surroundings of the cave as if it were moonscape. He must be up there watching somewhere, I thought, letting myself back down onto the string bed.

I lay back, studying the stars, getting my directions. The excitement was intense. Was this the chance I'd been waiting for? If he wasn't watching this would give me the head start I needed. Who knew when he would be back to check?

The excitement turned to fear and weighed on me heavy as lead. It was as though there was a rock in my stomach. 'Will he shoot if he sees me leave?' I pondered. It wasn't just a theoretical question. I was afraid as I had never been before. He'd have seen me when I stood up to look over the edge of the cut if he were watching, but he hadn't come down to reprimand me. No, it was too early to leave. 'If I go now,' I told myself, 'I'll be walking through villages in the middle of the night. The dogs will bark and people will think I'm a thief. People don't move around at one o'clock in the morning.' I would get either shot or caught. I'd have to wait till four o'clock at least. People started moving about by then, trying to make the most out of a day by using the last hours of darkness for travelling, getting the first stalls in the bazaar ready for the day's business, starting the fire in the *tandoor* oven that would have to burn for more than an hour before *naan* (flatbread) could be baked for breakfast. Four o'clock would be about right, even the mosque attendants would be on their way to sweep out the courtyards and make the call to prayer for the faithful.

The uncertainty and fear were paralysing. It would be so much easier just to stay put. Now the treatment was better, I even had a charpai, and I had got used to the routine. But what about my family? They are worried to death. The Mission might be trying to raise millions for my ransom. Had the ringleader said twenty lacs of rupees, or was I just imagining? Two million or whatever amount it would be, it couldn't be God's will for that money to be wasted, I reasoned with myself.

It struck me that something was happening to me, something I had heard about in hostages: I was starting to get used to this. That scared me. Could it be that I would lose my will to escape just because of the uncertainties escape entailed? Escape was holy. Escape, its possibility, its necessity, had kept me going. I couldn't give it up ever. What were these crazy ideas I was having? Why should I have to convince myself that I needed to escape? Or was I simply afraid? After all, at least I was alive . . . I didn't want to die, didn't want to get shot in the back while running down the ravine, didn't even want to get worse treatment because I had tried to escape. Yes, I was afraid. I admitted it to myself. That was it. That was bothering me. It was my basic survival instinct fighting against the drive to be free. Knowing that helped me to cope with my own fears and doubts.

The minutes seemed like hours, the moon was standing still. It had been an eternity since I had woken. I couldn't stand the pressure any longer. I had to do something. All this thinking, weighing the pros and cons wouldn't get me anywhere! I sat up and got my shoes, holding them like the key to my future. Once I'd got them on, the indecision and fear were gone. It was like diving off a ten-metre platform. Once you're in the air the fear is gone, there is no turning back, the decision in its finality carries one with it.

Now I could move. I headed down the hill, moving as quickly as the steep gradient would allow. In what seemed like just a few steps I was standing on the track where the car had stopped when the gang had brought me up here. As the clatter of stones rolling away as I dislodged them under my feet hadn't brought my guard down on me, I dared to stop and look back up the mountainside. I had got away undetected, I realized, standing still and listening. It seemed too good to be true. There was no shouting from above. No firing. No sound of movement, no rocks coming down to tell me I was being followed.

I struck out to the south-east, in the direction I had seen the lights from the top of the hill, but the track petered out after just a short way. I turned back frantically to try the other direction, painfully aware of the fact that I was still close to the cave, too close to the cave. I had to get away from here quickly, before the guard came back. My throat was dry with excitement, but I felt light, my steps easy. After walking briskly a hundred metres in the opposite direction it became clear that this just led back up the hill towards the house. It had to be the other direction. My first instinct had been right, I would have to find the track back there. Maybe it took a turn I had missed. I was wasting invaluable time, each second I dallied or squandered trying to find my way was time cut off my head start, time that might save me, time that could make the difference between escape and failure.

I scurried back in the other direction. The track had to go on, the vehicles that had made the scars on the face of the mountain had come along this way. They had to come from somewhere. Again the track petered out in the same place. After first fading into the unevenness of the gravel and sand, it had led me into a field of rocks and boulders that would make walking difficult, let alone getting a vehicle through. The thought never occurred to me that there might have been a rock slide covering it up since the gang had brought me in. Funny, our house in Canada had been built as a dwelling for a road worker who did nothing but clear the rocks off the road that came down the 'Big Slide' . . .

I couldn't see any way forward from here on. My conjunctivitis was bothering me, there was a film on my eyes and the moon was casting shadows and making weird reflections on the cliffs and boulders. I'd have to try further down the ravine, this had to be a side track after all. There had to be a way out of this place. Following the track back down, I came to a break in the boulders just wide enough to pass through. A path led through here: from the mouth of the cave I had seen a shepherd pass through here with his small flock, heading across the ravine towards the saddle path in the mountains opposite. Now, in the dark, it was impossible to see. There was just a steep drop. 'There must be a ledge along the side somewhere,' I reasoned, 'unless this isn't really the spot I saw. I can't make it out this way in the dark. Even if this does lead down to the dry wash at the bottom of the wadi, I can't go this way by night. It is too dark in the shadows of the cliffs. I can't even see to find my footing let alone keep it. It's no use, I'll have to go back.'

I felt foolish walking back and forth across the face of the mountain, right there for anyone to see. Would I find the cave again? What if I had already managed to get lost? How long had I been meandering like a fool? Two minutes? Twenty minutes? Even longer? Where was the cave? What would happen if I did find it and the guard came down just as I was returning? He couldn't have come back yet, otherwise I would have heard the ruckus that would be bound to ensue.

I struck out up the hillside again, trying to make the best of a botched job. The cave was right there, strange that I should find it so quickly when I hadn't been able to find the path down the valley! 'It must not be God's time yet for me to leave,' I deduced, dejected at having missed a chance, but relieved to have at least tried and to have not been caught. I'd just have to continue trusting him for consolation to my family, trust him to solve the problem of ransom the way he saw fit.

I couldn't sleep after the excitement, just lay wondering at the sense of it all. Wondering why I hadn't been able to escape. Wondering why I should wonder: was I worth it? Wondering at the majesty of the night mountain sky with its myriad of stars and my infinitesimal inconsequentiality in light of the expanse of the universe. I wondered. It was no wonder ancient peoples were so interested in astrology. The magnitude of the stars, the order of the cosmos, what is a human life in comparison with boundless space and spaceless bounds beyond? Was it not hubris, selfcentredness to think God might be interested in my plight? Yet he had bothered about me in the past, so many times.

Hadn't he just this week prevented my death by keeping the car from the crooks? Would they have spared me if they had got the car and its contents? They wouldn't have had to hang on to me as their only hope for some cash.

Captivity

The night as it bent towards the morning held a magical moment when time and space, the infinite and finite ceased to exist. Borne in a womb of fleeting insight I rested assured of the truth that God did care. He had let me fail to show me that he would take care of me in his own way. Perhaps there was a purpose to my being here that had not yet been fulfilled. I needed to wait, to wait on God.

Thursday 13th September, morning

As peace of mind came, so did sleep. I slept for about an hour until the dawn began to grey and my guard came. I chided him, jesting about his desertion on account of the mosquitos.

'I just go house one hour check on children,' he claimed.

'Did he really think I believed it? He must think I've slept the whole night like a baby! He really has no idea what I've been up to last night,' I reasoned. Relief swept over me. To think that I didn't know that he had not left just an hour ago to check on his household!

'Uttho!' He ordered me up from the charpai having undone the chains on my left leg. We moved the bed into the cave and I settled down for another long day. He didn't have any tea for me this time, and was gruffer than usual as he did up the chains again, fixing me to the charpai. I had the feeling I shouldn't have tried to crack jokes about the mosquitos. I sensed he could be cruel if caught in the wrong mood. There was no doubt about the vulnerability of my position. I had to be careful not to become too bold after last night's experience. Why hadn't he brought any tea this morning?

In spite of the bad taste left in my mouth from my guard's mood, it was luxurious having the charpai in the cave in comparison to sitting and lying on the ground. It lent dignity as well as a certain measure of comfort. Somehow it made sense that I should have it now after the failed escape, not before having tried. It was as if I needed it as I wasn't likely to get away soon. Did God want to encourage me? Make the wait for freedom more bearable?

Lying there on the cot in the cave, I tried to sort out my thoughts, tried to pray as I had the previous mornings, inspired by the break of a new day, humming or singing the morning hymns I had learned to value so deeply. It didn't work. I couldn't concentrate. 'It must be the lack of sleep last night,' I thought to myself. I tried to sleep, but all that came was a sort of stupor, a confused, disoriented and ill feeling.

I tried washing my face and neck with a few drops of water from the tin water pot as I had on previous days. It didn't make me clean, but did refresh a little. It helped for only a few minutes. As soon as I tried to apply myself to mental activity I found myself daydreaming or dozing. If I tried to sleep, the thoughts crowded my mind in a hopeless jumble. I felt unwell. Tired and weak, the makings of a headache, but not bad enough to be a symptom of oncoming malaria. I knew that from repeated experiences with the disease.

'Perhaps that's why God let me have the bed now,' I thought, 'I'm coming down with hepatitis. I shouldn't be surprised after the water I've been drinking; diarrhoea will be the next symptom, diarrhoea, vomiting and fever, from what I have seen others go through when they contract the disease . . . No, I'm exaggerating, it can't be hepatitis yet after just four days. I've got at least another week to get back home before the hepatitis hits.' The thoughts, confused as they were, brought a new sense of fear with them. Something else to worry about? Why then hadn't I been able to escape last night if my health was going to become a problem? I wondered how I would cope alone if diarrhoea and fever hit. That was something else I would just have to trust in God for, since there was nothing I could do about it anyway.

What if last night's failure was just to show me that it was possible to get away from the cave at night without being detected? Since I had the bed here in the cave now, I would probably be spending all the nights here. There would be other chances. If the guard left me alone last night, he would leave me alone again. Or had I spoiled my chances by suggesting to him that I knew he had been gone almost all night? On the other hand, I was still here, hadn't run away when I had the chance. He had no idea that I had tried. He would be careless again, think that I couldn't get out of the chains. That was it, he trusted the chains. Every day it was the same, he left me alone but chained up for hours on end. Unless there was someone, one of the boys posted further up the mountain to keep a lookout, that is. I would have to try to get a better look by daylight. I needed to know whether the cave was being watched. What about those signals, his waving his skull cap from the mouth of the cut to someone up the hillside? Was he bluffing, or had he really posted someone there? Anyway, I needed to get a better look down the mountainside by daylight too. If I were to get another chance to escape, I would have to know from the start how to find the path out of this canyon, which way to go. What was the sense in trying anyway, when the path just petered out . . . I had to get out . . .

It was no use, I couldn't get it together, couldn't concentrate. I could feel a strange numbness in the tips of my fingers. It couldn't be leprosy . . . I had to get control of myself, I was losing my grip on reality. Could it be that the sleeplessness of last night would have this devastating effect on me? The hours dragged on into the morning, the sense of frustration and confusion growing into the beginnings of panic. I had to do something, had to snap out of it.

That was it: I needed exercise. The motionlessness and the short night's sleep on top of it were taking their toll. I had had low blood pressure problems before when I'd been immobile for long periods, studying or working at my desk for days on end. The effects had not been this bad, but then I had never been chained up like this before, literally tied to one spot without any movement at all. I needed to move, needed to get my blood circulating. I'd have to exercise.

The experience last night had made me bolder. I took off the chains and did knee-bends, sit-ups, push-ups. It felt good to get the kinks out, good to sense the strain on my body, good to tire myself physically. The pain in my right shoulder was still there, but its edge was gone and I could manage even the push-ups. I pushed myself to the point of exhaustion, till my heart was pounding. Once my blood was circulating again at a normal rate, sleep came.

I slept well the rest of the morning, making up for sleep lost the previous night. It was midday when I awoke to the clatter of my guard's arrival. This time he had some bread and summer squash for me to eat. He set the food down to undo my chains. Since being without the chains was always a risk when he was gone, I decided to exercise some more while he was there. He got a kick out of the push-ups I was doing at the back of the cave.

'Yeah, a teacher,' he said half-loud with a knowing smile of recognition spreading over his face. Whatever the reason for his gruffness at dawn, he'd got over it in the meantime. He knew where to fit me in now: I was the schoolmaster who made the kids do exercises in school . . .

The sleep and exercise made me feel much better. The guard was in a visibly better mood so I decided to try some more small talk, maybe I'd find something out.

'Do you have a mosque here?' I asked, truly wondering where it might be: I hadn't heard a single *azaan*, the call to prayer, the whole time I had been held captive here. For that matter, I hadn't heard any the first day, Sunday, either, while I was confined in that hujra down in the village or town, wherever it was. Normally you couldn't miss the call to prayer. In the cities you heard several at one time. There was a system by which the muezzin farthest to the east started off, with those to the west chiming in as if they were singing together, but several beats later than the closest mosque to the east. In big cities like Lahore, with nearly five million inhabitants, there were so many mosques that the calls to prayer from a dozen different places of prayer were audible at the same time, the sheer number and volume of them obliterating the melody, creating an eerie wail, vibrating uneasily, making all but the nearest mosque's call unintelligible.

'Bazaar kay,' came the inevitable reply. If he meant the Jamrud bazaar two hours distant, then it was no wonder the *azaan* was not audible here. No wonder the people here didn't go to the mosque for prayers. At least that was the impression I got. I never saw any guard change into clean clothes and spruce up with a turban before leaving for town like villagers often do. But then he wasn't that sort of dignified man who wanted to be taken for a refined person. He was your basic mountain Pathan: a survivor, cunning, crafty, daring, tough, resourceful, proud, all of that and more, but not dignified or refined.

Captivity

Even if my guard were to go into Jamrud for prayers, he wouldn't be able to get home before it was time to leave again for the next *namaaz*. If he did offer *salaat* five times a day, he did it wherever he was, washing hands and forearms, face, eyes, ears, nostrils, mouth and feet for *wuzu*, the ritual purification before prayers, in the creek or with water poured from the well. If there was no water close by, using earth as the prescribed substitute for water was an alternative. Islam is indeed a religion conceived in the desert and suits these people's mentality as well as their environment, I thought.

'Do you go to the mosque?' I asked, just to keep the exchange going. You could hardly call it a conversation.

'Kal' – of course, he would go tomorrow, on Friday, for *Juma* prayers at midday. They were required for able-bodied men wherever there was an Islamic ruler.

'What's going to happen with me?' I came to the real topic.

'Kal.' Tomorrow he was going to the mosque, would meet people obviously, use the opportunity to find out as much as possible about the remnants of the gang that had kidnapped me. He would try to establish contact with them. It seemed he, too, had given up on them coming to say what was going to happen to me, or to take me somewhere else. They couldn't expect him to keep me for very long for 400 rupees. He must have been anxious to be rid of me. If the police connected the two who were killed on Tuesday with me, they might be able to trace me here.

My guard seemed bothered by thoughts about tomorrow. He rose from his haunches on the foot of the cot and did up my chains.

'Munga kar eshta Pikhawar kay? Chowkidari?' I couldn't believe it, was he really asking me for work in Peshawar? Did he want the job as gate watchman? It was unreal. How could he think that I would trust someone involved in my own kidnapping with my and my family's safety? This was just too much. Of all the cheek!

'We already have a chowkidar, and besides, I don't employ him, our landlord does. By the way, did you know that he is one of the biggest maliks in the whole province? You know, you really ought to let me go . . .'

He turned a deaf ear, gathered up the plate and bread basket in silence, hiding them under his chadar so that no-one would see he had been delivering food to someone and become suspicious. He didn't answer. How should that be interpreted?

After he left I thought about his request for a job. How must it have felt for him? It wouldn't have been easy. He must be desperate for income. Still, I just couldn't imagine using my influence to get him work. I couldn't do that to any employer. Nobody needed a crook in their ranks.

There was still no word from the thugs who were left from the original gang that had picked me up off the street.

The evening went with no-one coming or even sending a message. It was getting dark. Would anyone bring food for me tonight? My secret ration of bread was there in the chadar I had folded up into a pillow and was lying on. Eventually, he came without food.

'Uttho!' he said, having undone the chains. He led me out of the cave again, back up the ridge. But this time we didn't cut so steep an ascent, crossing the path to his house further down and going further out to the edge of the ridge at the opposite end from where his house was.

'Baittho!' He motioned for me to sit and dropped to his haunches as well.

'Hava' (air); he referred to the light, cool breeze sweeping down from the peaks surrounding us and rising up the ridge here in the middle of the valley. It felt so good after the stuffiness of the cave, where there was not even the slightest breath of air. We sat for five, maybe even ten minutes. I studied the upper reaches of the valley in the dusk intently. The dark, flat stretch between the ridge we were perched atop and the cluster of houses in the distance would be fields. Two lanterns showed up on the mountainside to the left. I followed them as they advanced like fireflies towards the cluster of houses where smoke lazily curled skywards from the cooking fires in the enclosed courtyards. The faint smell from the distant hearths was the smell of rural Pakistan: a sweet-pungent smoky fragrance produced by burning dung patties. The lanterns dropped from sight and my guard grunted for me to rise:

Captivity

'Uttho!' he ordered, putting an end to the reverie. We rose and skirted the ridge on the other side going back to the house, past the ruins of a house long collapsed and eroded, past the graves on the crest. Were these his family's graves? Children lost in birth or in infancy? Brothers killed in feuds with other villages and tribes? People were dying all the time. Life was hard here. No doctors, no hygiene. No health consciousness. No balanced diet. I tried to understand him, his people, the reasons behind their behaviour. Why he would keep me prisoner for just 400 rupees. Why change was so difficult in the tribal areas. Would I behave any differently if I were born and raised here?

We passed the small cow and the buffaloes chained to scrub trees and crossed the flat space that might serve as a threshing floor at harvest to the outer wall of the house. He had left the door ajar this time so he wouldn't have to call anyone. Didn't he want his own family, his wife and children to know he was keeping me in the house tonight? Or didn't they know at all that he was holding me prisoner? Did they think I had been a guest the first nights?

My guard had already given me to understand that he would be going in to town tomorrow. The problem still bothered him. He told me again before taking me into the house to sleep. I didn't think he would bring me back here since there was a bed in the cave now, but clearly it wasn't my comfort that was at stake, rather his ability to keep an eye on me. It was safer for him to keep me here, where he could sleep outside my door in peace and quiet without having to worry about whether I had broken out of the chains and escaped or having to fight off hordes of mosquitos. He was still afraid of me escaping, perhaps more afraid of what the gang would do to him than the police if they traced me here to his home.

My guard had to be careful that word didn't get out about me. He had to keep me under tight wraps, unlike the hostages kept openly in Afghanistan, free to move about in the village and mix with people because there was nowhere to go anyway and no-one to maintain law and order on the national scale.

Had I blown it this morning, raised his suspicions? It looked as if last night had been my one and only chance to escape by night . . .

There was no lantern tonight, so I ate by touch on the charpai in the dark room. It wasn't hard, as I ate with my fingers. I asked for water which was in the pot on the floor by the door: he guided my hand to it so I would find it more easily in the dark. I moved it against the bedpost. If he was going to chain me up again at least I would be able to reach it at night. He was. We went through the same routine, the only difference being that he was getting more practised and even deft at securing the lock.

'You don't need to put on the chains, you lock the door anyway!' I tried to reason with him.

'Need to.'

I didn't see any point in arguing. If I couldn't sleep, I'd take them off, they felt loose enough. On the other hand it was too risky getting woken up without them. Anyway, I'd been able to sleep with them till now, and I was especially tired after the previous night and the bad morning.

What were Marja-Liisa and the children doing now? Were they able to sleep? Were they as tired as I was? Where were they? At home? In Islamabad? They had probably left for Finland by now, the mission wouldn't let them hang in limbo for this long . . . But would Marja-Liisa be willing to go? Perhaps for the children's sake. How was she holding up under the strain? The only way to resolve the uncertainties and to find a measure of peace was to pray. If God was helping me to cope, he would be helping them too. The main thing was to stay in one piece, maintain balance, keep up hope and trust that God had a plan in this. I had to be glad that I was well, hadn't come down with any disabling illness yet. I was thankful I was feeling better now, prayed that my health would hold. I lay back and welcomed sleep as it came.

Friday 14th September, 4 a.m.

I awoke to the rattling of the door chain being unhooked outside. My guard opened the door and by the faint light filtering in through the doorway from the moon-washed courtyard undid my chains. He was quiet, simply motioning me to follow. We took the straight route across the plateau, along the path on the eastern side of the ridge and down the slippery, bare, stone, clay and gravel face of the mountain to the cut and the cave, stopping only for me to relieve myself. It was still night and too early for anyone to be moving about, I doubted whether anyone else in the house had been awake yet when we left.

'Baittho!' he barked. Without any further formalities he did up my chains and left. He was going to town today. What news would he bring back? Or would he bring people back with him? I didn't like the thought of that. I had learned to deal with this man at least a little. He wasn't exactly friendly, but hadn't been mean either. If others got involved, who could say what they would be like? If they belonged to the gang that had kidnapped me, they might want revenge for their two friends who had been shot.

Worrying wouldn't make the wait any easier. If one could only stop worrying just like that. Reasoning didn't seem to help when it came to any real-life existential crisis like this. There was no substitute for faith. My faith had enabled me to cope this far. The crisis yesterday when I had thought I was losing grip had passed. Somehow I felt I was being carried, supported. The dead weight and helplessness were there, but I didn't have to bear the weight alone. There must be people praying for me, I thought. At least family and friends would be, if they had heard the news. The people in Peshawar must have had word from the kidnappers by now, so at least they would know I was alive. I hoped that no-one would demand unequivocal proof of that. I didn't relish the idea of them sending a finger or an ear (which had happened to the Getty boy). What if the gang didn't make contact after the shooting incident? If they went completely underground? One of the ring-leaders, the one who had interrogated me had said that it was 'against their principles' to try and get in touch with the family of the victim. They waited until word was out and passed along the grapevine that there was interest in ransoming a missing person. The family of the kidnapped person would get in touch with some figure from the underworld and offer a finder's fee.

At least they hadn't been here, although my guard was expecting them to the point of distraction. He had been particularly curt this morning and visibly still nervous. The night's sleep hadn't changed anything, he had only spoken one word the whole way from waking me in the house to leaving me chained up in the cave, 'baittho'. It was his favourite word in Urdu.

Sitting is so important in this culture – sitting with people, not just sitting for sitting's sake. People have so much physical movement in this country that sitting has its own mystique. They walk everywhere. They bend, stoop, squat hundreds of times a day. Then there is the ritual kneeling, bowing, prostrating, rising repeatedly during daily prayers. There is a gracefulness about the way most people move in this part of the world. My guard had it too, that animal naturalness of being at ease with his body in contrast to the stiffness of westerners. You had a rest, shared a little comfort with another person, took a break. All that and more was involved in 'sitting' in this context. Every time I went to the bazaar someone was bound to say 'kayna kana', 'sit down, won't you!' Often I would be thankful for the chance, especially when it was in a bigger shop where we would sit on the floor bolstered up against big cushions with a chance to sit any way you liked: cross-legged, knees pulled up or feet stretched out. It wasn't only the 'sitting' either; the people made you feel welcome.

There was the old paint merchant in Saddar Lane off 'Fouwara Chowk', the 'Fountain Square' that neither had a fountain (any more, I guessed) nor was a square, but rather a circular opening between the bazaars. It was a major crossing, though. 'Chowk' also bore that meaning, as long as it was four streets being joined together. I passed him whenever I went to the fruit market or to buy oatmeal, tomato paste and – if he had it under the counter – the odd tin of 'it', ham (the word was never spoken as it officially didn't exist) from the wholesaler who had connections. I always had a bad conscience when I thought about passing the paint merchant, forever asking me to stop and sit with him when I went by his shop. I was always in a hurry, too rarely had 'time just to sit around' and do a missionary's real job, be with the people.

Captivity

He always remembered me from the time I had visited his shop and sat for a while discussing. It was two years ago now that I had bought paint from him for the house on Tariq Road we were then moving into. 'Apricot white' for the bedrooms, bright red to brighten up the rafters blackened with the years, white for the living room and kitchen, the rest was to be just whitewashed. If I had known that paint would peel where the brick walls were damp, I would have had the whole place just whitewashed . . .

I had had a couple of long discussions with the man when I went into his shop. He was a devout Muslim and wanted to know about the differences between Islam and Christianity, 'what could possibly keep me from embracing Islam as the final revelation of God's will through the prophets' . . . I really should have made more time to see him, like so many others I had had similar discussions with.

Friday, daybreak

The night turned to morning and, unlike the day before, I was able to enjoy the dawn breaking again. The play of colours in the roof of the cave flirted through the shades of violet, lavender, mauve, red, pink, peach, orange, sienna, ochre and sand as the rays gained intensity.

Lying on the charpai I was of course much closer to the roof of the cave. Turning my head to the opening to get a better view of the sloping roof as it dropped towards the back of the cave, I watched the insect life in the clay above come alive. There were minuscule spiders so small, I had never noticed them before. I wondered what they fed on, mites? Other microscopic organisms? The barren, apparently fruitless mantle of sand, shale, clay and rock was in fact full of life. I too was alive. In spite of everything I was alive. I had that to be thankful for.

The hymns were back with the sunrise. A new beginning by God's grace, by 'the great God's faithfulness', literally. That is what the Muslims say at every call to prayer too, '*Allah hu akbar* – God is greater, God is the greatest'. There is something we definitely agree on. Why is it that the faith in the one and only God expresses itself so differently?

'Great is thy faithfulness, O God my father . . .' no, no Muslim would ever think of saying that, that amounts to the arch-heresy, *shirk*, putting something or someone in the same category with God. Of course it is because we Christians believe in God as he revealed himself to us in Christ that it makes all the difference. Jesus made all the difference, just as he does in the various warring factions of Christian theology. It boils down to who Jesus is. It is part of the basic creed of Islam that 'God has no Son'. Muslims accept Jesus as the greatest prophet of all time until Muhammad, but not as God's Son, eternally begotten of the Father, conceived of the Holy Spirit. They do accept the virgin birth as a miracle, but cannot accept Jesus' death and resurrection. Not the new life in Christ by the power of the Spirit. Not salvation by grace. Not the categorically merciful God we know as Father.

Explaining these differences to a Muslim is not easy. It demands tact and at least a basic knowledge of Islam, so as not to offend the other, but even then it is a struggle. The issues are emotionally charged, with learned Muslims expressing their 'righteous' indignation and even fury at hearing such heresies. Is it really a sign of insecurity? Often such rigid and emotional positions are. The fact is, you have to experience it to believe it. Once you've experienced God's tender mercies, you're not willing to go back to a monolithic, unmoved God of the philosophers, a God so absolute he is absolved of every passion, unable to feel, unable to be moved, unable to suffer. A god so different from the God of Abraham, Isaac and Jacob. The God of the sunburnt, hardened, no-nonsense men of the desert. Strange that the Arab followers of Muhammad, so similar otherwise to the Hebrew patriarchs, had been inspired by such a distant God. It was certainly why Muhammad, after his death, had taken a position akin to that of Christ in Christianity in folk Islam.

'. . . Morning by morning new mercies I see . . .' As the hymn continued to sound in my ear, I appreciated it more and more. What kinds of experiences had led the authors of these hymns to be moved to the point where it had to find expression in art, in poetry and music, in the creative process? Whatever their experiences were, I felt united with them in my own tragedy. It was as if the hymns spoke for the first time to me here in the cave, directly, with no need for interpretation or application. It was almost as if they had been written for me alone, for me in my present situation. It was the feeling you had when some sentence in the Bible spoke, conveyed a message you felt no-one else could possibly understand, it was so personal and direct. A sense of being at the tangent point of time and eternity. It was 'joy' as C. S. Lewis defines it.

Each new morning had been saturated in mercy, God sustaining and protecting me, even allowing me the pleasure of enjoying the beauty of the sunrise as I saw it reflected in the clay of the cave. 'Thou changest not, thy compassions they fail not, Great is thy faithfulness, Lord unto me.'

If there is one thing that makes the Christian God different from the God of Islam, it is this. God is faithful, faithful to me, even though I might be unfaithful to him. He is not arbitrary, taking decisions at total random, saving or rejecting on a whim, sovereign in his independence from the need for justification of his doings. The Bible is a manifest of his love toward mankind. Though he may be 'Yahweh', the 'I shall be who I shall be', totally free and unbound by any philosophical necessity, he has made it clear in this manifest that he bound himself to love and faithfulness toward mankind. But it was in Jesus he bound himself to human flesh and so made his love and faithfulness truly manifest. In Jesus he had come to 'seek and to save' lost human beings, his creation, which had lost the image of its creator.

That was what had drawn one Muslim I knew well to Christ. He had been a *Molvi*, a religious leader, but couldn't find assurance of salvation, acceptance by God in Islam. He found it in Christ. In God's great faithfulness, in his unchanging compassion and faithfulness towards lost sinners.

I did my exercises and turned around on the charpai with my feet to the opening so I could see out of the mouth of the cave. There was less headroom this way, but it lessened the feeling of captivity and confinement to be able to see out into a wide open space. The sentinels were still there standing over the geometric designs on the face of the opposite mountain.

Friday, mid-morning

While the man was in town, the boys came to see me. I was able to talk with the Urdu speaker. He still pretended not to be involved at all. Who was to know, yesterday he was busy all day carrying rocks for building a new room, too busy to come and see me? Maybe he really was just here to help with the building. If he wasn't, he was paying a high enough price for an excuse to hang around. To go by the distant, but clearly audible sound of the rocks clanking as they dropped them, probably off the backs of donkeys, he was having to work pretty hard. Today there hadn't been any of those telltale intermittent sharp cracks and dull thuds. With the cat gone, the mice were at play. The boy was friendly enough, but also very interested in finding out about my financial resources, wanting to know if I had a car, what kind of car, the model, how much I paid rent, what my salary was. I spaced out his questions by ones of my own. I asked about the opposing slope and angular shapes sticking out of the grey mass of boulders, about the white lines horizontally delimiting the shapes.

'Sang-e-marmar' he said, matter-of-fact.

So they were marble mines, not some deserted village! The white line in the mountainside was where the marble vein surfaced. The dark blotches, the 'sentinels' weren't cypress trees but the mouths of the mine shafts. Without my glasses it was no wonder I hadn't worked it out. If there was mining going on over there, that would mean there would be trucks travelling at least that side of the valley! My heart began to race at the realization that there might be another way out of this place, a proper road to follow. I envisioned myself on the back of a truck huddling behind a huge marble boulder as the brightly painted and profusely decorated lorry with its curved bed groaned under the unjust treatment it was getting from such an oversized load.

Captivity

Truck drivers didn't seem to care too much how their payload weighed if it fitted on the bed or could be made reasonably secure from falling off, even though it didn't quite fit. Every time we drove to Lahore there would be at least one lorry along the route lying on its side having tipped over from loading too high. Often there would be one with a broken axle from too much weight. Our mission's driver had once explained that was why a truck would never give way on a narrow road, for fear it would roll on the soft shoulder or break an axle when the tyre dropped off the inevitably higher rim of the pavement.

That was it. From here I could get to the other side of the valley, and my guard would never expect that I had taken that route. Instead of trying to go down the ravine, I would go up it and cross the gulch where I had seen the shepherd boy disappear with his flock between the boulders and then reappear a couple of hundred metres further north in the bottom of the wash where the two lonely trees grew out of the dry river-bed. He had led his sheep up the opposite slope towards the saddle between two peaks. First I had thought that it might be my escape route, since Peshawar lay somewhere on the far side of the ridge opposite. Then I had discarded the plan as I had no idea whether it would be possible to traverse the far side. What if there were no paths, just a steep slope and loose shale and rock? This opened a whole new perspective: I would cross to the other side a little further up and then drop down into the other side of this valley beyond the low ridge just opposite my cave. I was already calling it 'my' cave. It was time to get away and this was the way!

'How many people work in the mines?' I asked, innocently enough, trying to establish something of the routine of the mines.

The answer was simple: the mines were depleted. They were closed, shut-down, inoperative, hopeless, depressing, useless to me and my hopes.

I tried to mask my disappointment, make small talk, ask for the Pushto words for things in the cave, limited and uninspiring as they were. He too, got tired of it and his efforts to size me up financially and left me to myself.

I exercised some more, then lay back for a rest.

Escape from terror

I heard someone approaching again, but this time it didn't come from the hill above. Almost as soon as the sound was audible, the little three-year-old boy, who had appeared naked at the cave with his seven-year-old sister a few days ago, came back with a woman in tow, climbing up into the cut from below right. They approached cautiously. The boy was dressed this time, wearing a dark brown shilwar-kameez. I remained absolutely still. I didn't know why. I could have called out for help, what harm would it have done me? I didn't know what to make of it. They stood in the cut leading to the cave for a long time, peering into the dark recess trying to see me, see who was in there. Was it the man's wife and son? Were they taking the opportunity while he was gone to see what this was all about? I reasoned that the boy or his sister must have told his mother when they had seen me. Was the mother, a stocky woman of indeterminate age between thirty and fifty – women aged faster here with their heavy work load and hard life – just curious, or was there more to it? She had the front of her *burqa* thrown back over the crown of her head so I could see her face. That was odd. Maybe she knew I was a foreigner. Foreigners weren't really men, at least they weren't dangerous, so she didn't have to be afraid of showing her face. Was that it, or was it just that she had to lift the veil to be able to see into the darkness of the cave against the glare of the mountainside? Could she see the chains on my feet? They were stretched out towards her. If she could see anything, that would be the first thing she would make out. Eventually they left. It seemed an age that they had been looking at me like an animal in the zoo.

Today my condition was better, the exercise was helping. A verse from Paul's letter to Timothy that I had read together with the new bishop came to mind: 'Bodily exercise profiteth little'. These things need to be seen in context: I was profiting a lot, my spiritual vitality depended on it. Then again, the amount of walking Paul himself did travelling through Asia Minor and Greece would have been more than ample exercise. He didn't write postcards or take the bus. He would have been in even better shape than the normal lithe and supple Pakistani villager today. Paul the Apostle obviously meant the obsession hellenistic Greeks and Romans of his day had with the athletic body of a young god.

Friday, midday

The day dragged on. The boys brought some bread and *kali thorri* squash at lunch time. They sat down to watch me eat.

'Won't you join me?' I asked, gesturing to the small cup of squash as cultural dictates required.

'Thank you, we have already eaten,' the elder of the two across the cave from me replied, equally bound by dictate to refuse when only such a small amount was available. Who was to know, maybe they had already eaten?

'So the man hasn't come back?' I queried.

'After prayers.'

Of course, since he was in town, he would attend *Juma* prayers as every Muslim should. That was probably why he went today: anyone he wanted to see would be likely to be there at the mosque for the Friday midday prayers. He could ask around unobtrusively, meet people 'by chance' without arousing any suspicion. I was sure he was desperate to hear from the thugs himself. My kidnappers had promised him 400 rupees to keep me for one night and the next day. At least they had said they were returning the very next day when they had left me on Sunday evening.

My stomach had shrunk so much that it wouldn't take much food at a time. The bread was yesterday's and, though not tough and hard yet, didn't inspire me to eat as much as I could. I finished my meal and the boys gathered the bread basket and the cup and went back up the hill.

I tried to listen for the call to prayer from the mosque. The time passed so slowly. I couldn't have missed it if it were audible. It hadn't been time yet when the boys left. Surely it must have passed by now, the sun was well past its zenith. 'Zenith', that was an interesting word in European languages: an Arabic word. When Europe had been in the dark ages, the Muslim world had been technically and scientifically very advanced. Scientific terms from the fields of astronomy and mathematics, like 'zenith' and 'algebra', were adopted directly from the Arabic into the European languages. Similarly, Aristotle's complete works, lost to European academics, were re-translated back into the Greek from the Arabic translations the Moors and other Muslims introduced to Christian scholarship. Muslims were rightfully proud of their academic heritage. Many Muslims I knew rebelled inwardly against the forces in Islam that had cast an image of a less civilized and accomplished people than their forebears. The burning of Baghdad was viewed as the most barbaric act of recorded history. With it, in their opinion, Islam had been cast into its own dark ages. They viewed the rise of fundamentalism as a disaster for Islam. They couldn't be very vocal about it, though. The repressive atmosphere was not conducive to criticism, no matter how constructive it was meant to be.

The silence of the midday heat shouted from the hard-baked earth and echoed from the mountains and sky. The nearest mosque must have been truly far away, completely out of ear-shot. It was a strange feeling realizing that. Again I reflected that it was the first time I could remember having been in a place for any length of time where the call to prayer in this Islamic state could not be heard. It was remarkable how difficult it was to get out of the reach of the muezzin. That was obviously what at least one faction of the founding fathers had wanted when they demanded that a separate, Islamic state be carved out of a part of India when the British granted independence. They had wanted the high religious profile inherent to the traditional image Islam has always had where it had been the majority or ruling religion. They could not be content with a situation in which religion was a private, personal matter along the lines of dominant western concepts such as the 'secular democracy' idea propagated by the Indian Congress Party. *Dar-ul-Islam*, the house of Islam, yearned for an outward form and appearance, for the theocracy proclaimed by the Prophet. Other factions had other interests, some very secular. Jinnah, the 'Father of the Nation', and many of his political consorts had not had the idea of an Islamic society ruled by religious norms as represented in the *shariah*. But once a separate state for Muslims had been founded, its whole raison d'être hung on raising the Islamic profile. Shariah law, a shift to a two-class society characterized by a ruling Muslim majority and a 'protected' that is subjected *ahl-e-dhimma* composed of those who did not convert to the majority religion, Islam, had forced itself upon Pakistan as it had so many other Islamic states. A growing sense of intolerance toward liberal-minded Muslims was the inevitable outcome.

Friday, afternoon

For a hundredth, if not the thousandth time I tried to resolve what was happening, what my family knew, where the rest of the gang were, what would happen next. What I could do, what I should do. My guard had still not returned from town. Perhaps he had met up with the gang this time. Were they coming back together? Did he have to wait for them in town until they were ready to leave? Or hadn't he found them? Was he still trying to locate someone who could give him information of their whereabouts? The long, hot afternoon was excruciating in its silence. Again it seemed as if the sun stood still. Nothing happened to make the clock tick. There was no clock. Time was imaginary. Life hung still, dangling from an invisible thread like a spider, motionless on its web. For the moment there was only waiting, waiting and praying.

Late in the afternoon the man came back. His dark face wore an even blacker expression. He hadn't found anything out. Said he'd go back again tomorrow. He was nervous. He offered me an Urdu daily newspaper I'd never seen before, *Shahadat*, coming out of Peshawar, but carrying almost no news. It was just a few pages of nothing of any importance. It didn't even have a crime page, no mention of any missing foreigner. Still, it was a nice gesture to bring me a newspaper. He hadn't bought it for himself. He couldn't even speak Urdu, let alone read it.

There was no news about me. I had to admit to myself, that that was all I cared about at the moment. I wondered what that meant. Was it just a crummy paper? Was I already old news? Was there a restraining order from the court not to report so as not to endanger negotiations? Had the police kept a lid on it? Or didn't they even suspect that I had been kidnapped? What were they thinking? Or was I thinking along erroneous lines? Maybe I just wasn't a news item. What was one foreigner in a country with 120 million people and more problems than could be numbered?

Friday, dusk

At dusk he brought me food. Would I be spending the night in the cave again? Normally I ate after he moved me up to the house. He told me to pull my foot out of the chain. I was taken aback. Had the boys told him how we had laughed about how sloppily they were fixed? I motioned for him to undo them. He yanked at them until they were loose enough to pull off and walked off into the dusk. Did he want me to run away, or did he simply realize that I could have at any time already and still not done so? I ate my meal. It was *dal*, grams, similar to lentils. After the bread and simple vegetables it tasted almost like meat! I saved a piece of bread in case I did get a chance to escape this evening when it was dark, or if not, for the morning. I never got any breakfast.

It was a peculiar feeling sitting there unchained waiting to see if he was coming back, a naked sort of feeling. The voices of a man and woman quarrelling at the tops of their voices drifted down from the ridge. It was the first time I had heard human voices while alone in the cave. Just after dark I heard him approaching. Did he want to see if I had taken the first opportunity to escape? Seeing me still there he motioned me to follow. I couldn't read any surprise in his face or voice at my still being there. I rose quickly from the string bed I was sitting on and almost forgot to pick up my shirt and trousers. I had been using them as a pillow, wrapped up in the chadar. My guard struck out down the slope without waiting to see if I was following. I groped for my shoes under the bed, trying to slip into them as I began to move out of the mouth of the cave.

He led the way down the mountainside to the same track I had tried Wednesday night, actually Thursday morning. So it had been the right track after all. We turned to the right as I had done intuitively that night. Before we got to the place the track petered out he turned off to the left, winding through the boulders. I couldn't see where the path went in the dark. I stuck to his heels. This path would be just as hard to find, if I ever had the chance to try to escape at night again. Where were we going? Was he taking me to another hiding place? Was it getting too hot for him having me so near his house? Had he heard bad news in town today? If so, why would he be going back tomorrow?

Perhaps that was his wife who had seen me today. They had been fighting while I ate, it had been their shouting I could hear all the way down to the cave. Did she want him to get rid of me? Or did she want him to let me go? Had the neighbours heard the fight, was the secret out? Was that why he was moving me to another hide-out? Or was he leading me to freedom? The excitement swelled until I was saturated with the adrenalin it produced. I sensed a total alertness I had not known before. The sound of the stones crunching under our feet rang out with such volume to my over-sensitive ears that I felt the whole valley must hear our movements.

We walked on without speaking for a quarter of an hour. Somewhere along the way we emerged from the boulder-strewn, seemingly un-navigable landscape back onto a broader track like the one we had started out on. Further down, two lights appeared on the mountainside ahead of us. My guard motioned for me to climb up the mountainside and press my white face against the rock. We waited, not moving, until two people passed. He didn't want to be seen, anyway, wherever he was leading me. We were on a beaten path again, wide enough for the car to have used when it brought me up here. Then, abruptly, we turned off the path again, this time to the right, circumventing the base of a ridge. He dropped to a crouch motioning for me to do the same while he scouted the lie of the land on this side of the valley below him. I wondered if this were the beginning of the ridge his, and the other one or two houses were perched on. The lie of the land was more complicated than I had even imagined.

Assured there were no movements in the darkness ahead, he rose, motioning me to follow. It seemed so natural, and yet at the same time unbelievable that real people behaved like stalking animals. Another fifteen, twenty minutes passed before we reached the bottom of a hill with a large house perched on the crown. He motioned for me to sit beneath a scrub tree and went up to the house. He was there for a long time. Beneath me were irrigated fields surrounded by a line of trees. That would be where the water flowed. Judging by the fields, this man was far more well-to-do than my guard. He probably had a couple of acres of irrigated crops here. I wondered if I were to run down the hillside and follow the irrigation channels, if that would lead me out of here. I prayed for help and guidance to know what to do. It seemed as if an hour had passed since the man left me here. What in the world could be keeping him this long? Finally, he returned with another man. It was a tense moment . . . I didn't know what to expect. Was this one of the gang who had kidnapped me? Why had my guard brought him down to see me? The second man looked me over and said with the voice of authority: 'he's an Afghan, let him go!'

I could hardly believe my ears! They continued discussing, arguing about who should let me go, obviously neither wanting to bear the responsibility. The man who lived in the big *kor* on the hill appeared to be a local chieftain, a *malik*, who could provide protection for my guard should there be any reprisals against him for having released me. Finally they jointly agreed to let me go.

We rose and they led the way across the scrub hillside between the huge clumps of bunch grass to the track we had departed from further up the valley.

'Baittho!' I wondered what this was about, but sat down, as commanded.

'This is the road,' said the *malik*, patting the path with his hand as if it were listening to the same set of instructions I was about to receive. 'Stay on it. Don't turn anywhere, left or right. Walk for two hours and you will come to the city, to Jamrud. Wait there till four o'clock. Four o'clock in the morning the gate opens and a wagon will depart for Peshawar. You will be home by morning.'

He reached into his breast pocket and gave me ten rupees for the fare.

'Fare is four rupees. You can get a cup of tea in Jamrud while you wait for the bus to depart.'

I was itching to get started, yet unsure whether I should say anything. I didn't like the idea of hanging around Jamrud, famous for its organized crime and smuggling syndicates, in the middle of the night. I didn't expect there to be many nice people up and about at that time, but what alternatives did I have? If I could only skirt the city and get to the Peshawar road. Best not to show I was so excited.

'Dawa karo!' he commanded, half Pushto, half Urdu.

It took a moment to register. He had asked me to pray for them! Why should he do that? He couldn't have meant 'daawa karo' – 'preach to us!' I had been able to say hardly anything about my Christian faith to him. It could only be the Pushto corruption for 'du'a karo', 'pray'. Perhaps it was because I had prayed for the widows and orphans of the men who had been shot. The fact that they had done me harm hadn't hindered my praying for them. Perhaps he thought he came under the same category, that I wouldn't bear a grudge.

That still didn't explain why he wanted me to pray for him. Had I been able, in some way I didn't realize myself, to be a witness to Christ, to make an impression on him? There was no time to think, the men already had their hands out with palms upturned waiting for the prayer . . .

'Loving, merciful God, bless these men. Bless their children, give them health and strength, bless their fields, that there will be food for their families and livestock. Lord, bless their animals, the buffalo, cows, donkeys, goats and chickens. Keep them from harm and let them multiply in blessing for these men who are now releasing me. Lord, I pray that you would let them see the light that drives out all darkness of the heart, in Jesus' name, amen.'

I truly wished that God would bless them and theirs. The greatest possible blessing would be a new life following Christ. I had no sooner finished than my guard said in his mixed languages:

'Man who prays, go!'

My guard took back his chadar. It was still useful and probably of value to him; it wasn't even torn anywhere, unlike the suit of clothing he had given me. The piece of bread I had hamstered fell out of the chadar as I unravelled my own clothes from it, but they didn't notice. In the dark I couldn't find it. I would have to manage the journey without any food. What about his clothes I was wearing? I desperately needed them! I asked him about them.

'Bakshish,' he replied. I could keep them. I asked him if he wanted my clothes in exchange and realized how ridiculous that was before he could reply in the negative.

I turned my back on them and the past. Below and ahead lay a new life.

FREEOM

Friday, 8 p.m.

'Man who prays, go!' I was buoyed up by the knowledge that this was God's timing. This explained why I had not succeeded in escaping on Wednesday night, why I had had no other opportunity. God had known the way out for me, he had prepared it all the time I was worrying. 'The Lord is my shepherd, I shall not want. He leadeth me . . .' He would show me the way now too.

As the track opened before me I felt hope and courage well up from somewhere deep inside. There was a confidence that had been missing on Wednesday. Of course there was a simple difference, I didn't have to worry about anyone chasing after me! Being able to concentrate simply on the way forward and what lay ahead made the going much easier. The going was much easier here. We had already left the more difficult part behind us on the way to this night encounter. I could see the general lie of the land before me as it dropped away towards a ridge traversing the bottom of the valley.

The path zigzagged back and forth on the long descent. Soon the valley widened out and the incline became less steep, the path straighter. I walked as if carried on wings. There were no dwellings or signs of habitation for the better part of an hour. That agreed with what one saw of Pathan country when flying over these barren mountain ranges: there were settlements and fields on the flattened crests of the lower mountains and in the high valleys and also along the fringes of the mountain ranges these proud and indomitable people called home. I was still in the area in-between which was badly eroded by flash flooding and over-grazing. Judging by the slope of the incline, though, it would not be long before I came into the area where the flow-off from the floods slowed enough to be caught behind dikes where the water could soak into the ground, making it fertile and sustaining the crops eking an existence out of the meagre mixture of rocks, sand and clay.

As the kilometres passed and I began to calm down somewhat, the mountains surrounding me, growing ever higher in relation to my descent, brought to mind Psalm 121. Perhaps it wasn't the mountains, but the ease with which I had been making headway that it accompanied me in such a tangible way:

> I lift up my eyes to the hills –
>> where does my help come from?
> My help comes from the LORD,
>> the Maker of heaven and earth.
> He will not let your foot slip –
>> he who watches over you will not slumber;
> Indeed, he . . . will neither slumber nor sleep.
> The LORD watches over you –
>> the LORD is your shade at your right hand and;
> the sun will not harm you by day,
>> nor the moon by night.
> The LORD will keep you from all harm –
>> he will watch over your life;
> the LORD will watch over your coming and going
>> both now and for evermore.

Still, I was worried. What would it be like without the promise of this psalm, without the knowledge that I was not alone? I hated to think. So much uncertainty lay ahead. What would happen when I got into the inhabited area? Would I have to talk my way around anyone? I loathed the thought. I didn't know enough Pushto to pass for a Pathan. Should I try to fake it with Farsi, pretending I was an Afghan refugee from an area of Afghanistan where the Persian dialect, not Pushto, was spoken? It would almost be better to pretend I was a deaf

Freedom

mute. I had learned to 'sign' a little the primitive way most of the untrained disabled did here, with the deaf and dumb labourer working on the construction gang that had built most of the structures I had supervised on behalf of the mission and the church. It was pretty graphic: 'eat' was all five fingers of the right hand joined together almost touching the lips. 'Drink' was holding the cupped right hand in front of the chin and raising it just a tad. 'Pain' was slowly clenching a fist with the palm pointing upward and squinting at the same time. It would be definitely easier to fake than Farsi or Dari – I only knew a few words, mostly greeting formulas.

The best solution would be just not to run into anybody! If that could only be achieved . . . I would have to find a way around Jamrud. I tried to imagine what the outskirts of the city would be like: large, rectangular, high walled enclosures of about half an acre, some more, some less. The mud walls were between four to six metres high. On the corner where the actual living quarters were built up against the mud walls, there would be a guard tower with small shooting slits covering the length of two sides, in one of which would be the huge iron gate. In some cases there might be a second tower diagonally to the other so that all outside walls were covered. Here, a man's home truly was his castle, and a fortified one at that. Feuds continued for generations in some instances. One always had to be prepared against surprise attacks. I could probably avoid them. Since there were no windows in any of the walls except for the shooting slits in the watchtowers, I wouldn't be seen from any of these *kors* unless, for some reason, there was a watchman on duty in the tower or at the gate. In the dark no-one would be able to make me out anyway, if I kept my distance. The guard dogs might be a problem though. I prayed that a way would open up for me, so that I would not have to enter Jamrud. If there were any 'nice' people in this area at all, the bazaar of this notorious drug and smuggling centre after midnight wouldn't be the time and place to find them!

The track descended the mountainside to the bottom of the wadi and fused with the dry river-bed. Here and there were puddles of stagnant water and clumps of small trees. Down in the river-bed moving became more difficult. In the shadow of the trees I could no longer see where the puddles lay and walked into one. Very soon after I realized I was going to have to get my feet dry quickly if I wanted to avoid getting blisters. I took off my socks and wrung them out. I walked on without them until the squishing of the water in the leather in my shoes stopped, at which point I put my socks back on.

Houses were scattered here and there now, dogs barked at my passing, but no-one was moving about. This was different than I had expected. I couldn't skirt these settlements. To do that I would have to climb the mountain as the enclosures were situated, quite under-standably, up the hillsides away from the danger of floods in the wadi. Were these even the outskirts of Jamrud? I didn't think I had been walking quite two hours yet.

In the total darkness I had to look back at times to find the track and draw an imaginary line forward from what was visible behind. It was more visible in the light reflected from the stars by the barren mountainside looming behind me. The valley narrowed here. I thought it would have to widen and spill out into the plain of 'Ghandahara', that ancient centre of Buddhist culture that had flourished here until the Pathans, then known as Parthians, and other marauding Aryans invaded the subcontinent about the time their distant cousins the Goths and Vandals were harassing the very heart of the Roman Empire. But the valley got narrower and narrower with no sign of the plain opening up ahead. As the valley narrowed it also began to twist and turn as it found its way between lower hills and crowding in from both sides. It was no longer as easy going as it had been. 'My Lord knows the way through the wilderness, all I have to do is follow'. The song I had learned as a child in Sunday School came back to encourage me as the going got tougher.

The dry wash turned left, and coming out from behind a stand of trees I saw the first light bulb, hanging from a wire in front of what looked like the entrance to a mine shaft in the side of the hill, not far above the bottom of the canyon. As I held to the left edge of the wadi, opposite the shaft I came to a large, well fortified house enclosure on the hillside to the left and across the track from where the light hung.

Freedom

No light was visible in the house, but then there wouldn't be, seeing that there were no windows in the perimeter wall. A dog barked and soon another joined in, but I was quickly out of sight and kept going at the fast pace I had been keeping up all along.

It was the only light for at least another half hour. Against the faint horizon on the crest of the hill to the right there was a huge enclosure, but not the faintest glimmer of light spilling over the walls. It was somehow ominous and threatening as I passed beneath it. The excitement began to return with the enhanced possibility of running into someone on the path or stumbling onto someone's property and waking up the dogs. It wasn't too late yet for the odd person to be returning home from the city, although all the local people would be indoors by now if they had spent the day in the vicinity.

I thought of the traffic on the roads of Pakistan: the hour just after dusk was the worst. The twilight was dim in these latitudes, and all the men on bicycles, the ox carts, droves of donkeys used as beasts of burden at construction sites, herds of goats and sheep, milking cows and huge, black buffalo which were more than a match for any car should it come to a test of destructive power in a collision, all added up to a terrible brew on the street. If I had to travel by car after dark I usually tried to start the journey after 8 p.m. when all the bicycles and animals would be off the streets. On this track I didn't suppose more than a few cars a week would pass. Hadn't the redhead mentioned that a pickup came part of the way every day though? At least, it would on days it didn't rain and that was almost every day. Besides, the whole country went to sleep when it rained. The streets flooded from inadequate or blocked sewage lines, the dirt roads turned to mud. The shopkeepers couldn't put their wares out on the street in front of their *dukans*, little cubicles behind rolling steel shutters so crammed with goods it was impossible to do business unless the shopkeeper made room for himself to stand by lifting merchandise racks and crates out onto the street. Even many schools stayed closed on rainy days.

Turning out of a hidden curve in the track I again saw an electric light straight ahead. With the bright light in the distance it was easier to make out the path with the contrast of light and shadow. There were tyre tracks now, ruts in the river-bed. Cars used this as a road even if most of the traffic here would be on foot. Perhaps I was getting close to Jamrud. The dry river-bed was some twenty metres across at this point, with dense foliage on the left bank and village-type houses with lower walls and smaller enclosures beginning to fill up the right bank. That was where the light hung from a tree, under which the men of the village sat on their charpais discussing and trying to get relief from the heat stored up in the houses during the long, hot day.

What should I do? It didn't seem a good idea to follow the direction of the road through the bush on the left. I would be bound to make a lot of noise snapping twigs and stumbling on roots. It would be difficult to explain why I was trying to sneak past if the men noticed me anyway. On an impulse I walked straight ahead with no slacking of my brisk pace. Keeping to the shadows of the trees and bush on the left edge of the river-bed, I skirted the circle of light thrown by the single bulb. Keeping my face fixed straight ahead, I strained my eyes to widen my field of vision. I wanted to see whether the men noticed me pass by. I must have been just a fleeting shadow in the dark grey shilwar kameez beyond the perimeter of their vision, as I could register no glance in my direction, although I passed within fifteen metres of them, picking up their small talk and laughter as I hurried on.

Friday, 9.30 p.m.

Passing out of the light flooding the centre of the small village I lost the track. Walking away from the light was like walking into a pitch black tunnel. I slowed my step and felt the heat in my thighs and the beginnings of stiffness from the ten to fifteen kilometres I had come downhill as fast as I could walk. I checked the floor of the wadi from edge to edge for some sign of traffic when my eyes became reaccustomed to the darkness. I looked for another section, ruts in the river-bed, but not even stooping in the darkness and trying the surface with my hands brought any worn path. The wadi had widened out again and was strewn with fist-sized rocks, gradually growing in size as I moved along. I didn't want to go back. It was fortunate enough that they hadn't seen me and if they had, to have suspected nothing the first time. What were the alternatives? This was a dry river-bed, it would lead out of the mountains wherever it went as it sought lower ground. Eventually it would meet up with the Kabul river, but before that, most likely, Peshawar's lights would be visible in the distance.

The going got more difficult as the size of the rocks littering the river-bed increased. Picking my way through them I came up against a sheer rock cliff, which turned the river off to the left, whenever it carried water. Now, a month after the monsoon season had ended, there were only pools of water in the depressions and in places like this where there had been a natural blockage of the flow, enabling the parched and hardened earth to drink its fill. Soon after the bend, the bottom of the valley gave away all at once in a jumble of outsized boulders the torrents had swept along in their unimaginable fury. I was thankful now that my prayers for rain had been answered in the negative . . . it would have been a sheer impossibility to traverse this terrain had there been even the slightest rain. Walking turned to climbing as I picked my way down the cascade, wondering if I was just getting deeper into trouble all the time.

It was clear now why the path had petered out where the men had been sitting. This route was impassable for all intents and purposes. The track must have passed right through the middle of their charpais, leading up the hill on the right, crossing it and dropping down into another valley. By the glow on the horizon to my right beyond the crest of the ridge crowding the river-bed I could tell I was circling Jamrud as I had hoped and prayed I would! At the bottom of the cascade the river-bed was a mess of litter and deep furrows between long ridges of gravel the monsoon floods had ploughed into the landscape. Climbing in and out of the furrows there was no way to keep my feet dry. My shoes had dried out once already, they would dry out again.

On the right bank I found a narrow footpath that rose out of the jumble of gravel, driftwood and rock to higher ground, following the general course of the stream. Rising over a low crest, a light became visible directly on the path. The warm yellow light of the incandescent bulb gave a sort of sheen to the small mud house outside which it hung. I approached warily, trying to establish whether anyone was up and about. Treading carefully, so as not to make any noise, I neared the building. As I drew nearer I could see that there were two buildings. What had appeared to be an extension of the hut from a distance was actually a small, separate room, maybe a stall for goats or a buffalo. As I passed it, I could see that the door to the living quarters was open and only the obligatory 'purdah' curtain or veil hanging listlessly in the still and hot night air. Stepping off the path to the left I scurried down the hill into the darkness and security of the river-bed. To my surprise and great relief the river-bed had flattened out and I picked up a new track.

There was no sign I had alerted anyone in the house, but across the wash a pack of dogs barked furiously as I descended. They must have been tied up though, or behind some sort of fence, because their barking didn't come any closer. Further on, the river-bed flattened out even more and was almost a hundred metres wide. There were no boulders here, just sand and gravel, the flow-off from flash floods losing its momentum as the valley widened and the gradient lessened. Off to the right, I guessed it must be west or south-west, the ridge was much lower, really only a slight incline in the landscape, and the light above Jamrud was no longer visible. Had I already passed it? Was I going off in the wrong direction altogether? On the left dogs barked again. As I drew closer, I could see that the trees growing along the left bank were evenly spaced, an orchard of some sort, surrounded by a fence. The dogs were there to protect the trees, a common enough practice. They could be fierce. The son of the abdicated King of Swat State, now part of the North West Frontier Province of Pakistan, its mountain 'paradise', had once asked us to tea when we, on a holiday, walked by his home. He warned us not to wander into the forest as he had particularly fierce Tibetan mastiffs roaming the woods at night to 'discourage' people from cutting his forest for firewood. Well, these

Freedom

dogs wouldn't bother me as they were behind the fence. Nor did it seem there were any dwellings in the area, so there was no need to be alarmed by the barking.

Passing the tip of the plantation, I could see that I was in a wide valley now. The ruts and tyre tracks dispersed in all directions making it impossible to know which ones led where I needed to go. I was covered in sweat, tired and thirsty, but I simply plodded on keeping more or less to the middle of the wash, my feet mechanically beating pace according to some inner clock.

My eyes filled with tears as the children's song we sang as a lullaby to Anna picked me up and carried me onward: 'A child's path leads through the wilderness, but a wonderful angel shows the way home. The way is so long, home is not to be seen, but the wonderful angel walks alongside . . .' In an inexplicable way, the song gave me strength to plod onward. I felt God's angel walking with me, watching over me. It couldn't have been a mistake, not turning back when I had lost the track. I had to believe it, believe that I was being led out by the way right for me. At least I had not wound up in Jamrud. That was what I had been most afraid of. As long as there were vehicle tracks, I was getting closer to some road.

Something didn't fit into the desert night. What was it? It was a sound and as I progressed it became discernible. Music – it was western music. Voices were speaking in some foreign language . . . it was English! Where in the world was it coming from? Was I hallucinating? As the sound rose to a crescendo its source became visible: a huge white enclosure standing alone on the right bank. Judging by the tracks in the sand any number of cars must have driven into the enclosure. It was a party of some sort, I guessed. The attraction was a 1950s American film being shown against the high, whitewashed wall of the house inside the courtyard. I could just see the top of the frame over the surrounding wall. Not knowing whether people would be coming and going, I hurried past. It seemed to be a lone house. No others were in sight, but who could tell what might be just a hundred metres away? I wondered if it was one of the infamous drug barons' mansions. One of the more famous had acres of lawns, swimming pools, a golf course and a completely air-conditioned palace complete with lift and its own electricity supply.

Friday, 11 p.m.

I had been walking steadily for at least three hours now and it was only supposed to take two hours to the city. Were these isolated houses actually the outskirts of Jamrud, or had I strayed off in a completely different direction? I had no way of knowing. My eyes had been blindfolded when the gang had brought me in the car, with the exception of just a couple of minutes when we had entered the mountains and the ringleader sitting next to the driver had called out 'Waziristan zindabad!' trying to fool me into thinking we were a couple of hundred kilometres further south.

They had succeeded, at least initially. Now something loomed ahead in the darkness that helped me to understand why I had needed to be un-blindfolded for just those brief moments: looming before me was the aquaduct I had seen coming into the mountains. There was no doubt about it even though I was looking at it from the other direction. The bad leak on the east end of the water bridge, carrying irrigation water from a canal four metres above the floor of the valley across to a continuation canal on the opposite slope, sealed the fact. This is the right way out! Without having the faintest idea where I was going, I had taken the shortest possible route along the edge of the mountain range, by-passing Jamrud at the same time. Now the question was, where to from here? While I thought it over and tried to reconstruct the topography in my mind, I climbed up the slope to where the leak was splashing to the ground. I took off my shoes and socks, stepped under the gush of water, and quenched my thirst drinking directly from the waterfall. For a few minutes I let the water flow over my head and shoulders. As an afterthought I wet my clothes standing under the fist-sized hole in the cement aquaduct. That would keep me cool a little longer. The forceful shower worked wonders, cooling me off and refreshing me. I wondered whether it was wise to drink the river water straight from the canal, but I didn't really have a choice. I had been sweating so much I would have soon become dehydrated. Anyway, I had been drinking impure water all week.

Thinking it through, I decided I wouldn't turn off to the left at the big puddle. It lay in front of me fed by the leak I was showering in. That was where we had come from by car. I distinctly remembered traversing the puddle and turning right under the low bridge. We had followed the irrigation canal for a few minutes prior to that, but they had opened my blindfold at a spot where they were on no track at all, crossing a rolling, gravel moonscape. It was no use going that way. It would be best just to continue following the lowest land, the river-bed.

Putting my shoes and socks back on, I scrambled back down the slope. A hundred metres further down the valley a car's lights appeared on the left. It crossed the wash and disappeared on the far side. I set out in that direction. Here, again, were all kinds of vehicle tracks. In the day-time this would be a well-used route although not officially a road. Much of the tribal area is travelled in this manner, pickups the conveyance of preference because of their high ground clearance and one can easily fit twenty people on a pickup, and whereas the 'wagon' drivers did their best to cram as many into a Ford Transit or Toyota Hiace van, the walls and the roof put a ceiling on their ambitions.

Houses were more regularly spaced out now, every couple of hundred metres. One on the far side of the wash, which was a couple of hundred metres wide here, had blue-green lights strung along the edge of the roof. Did that have anything to do with the belief many Muslims share, that evil spirits shied away from the colours blue and green because they hated water and would be fooled into thinking a house painted blue or green was actually water. Most people are preoccupied with the effects of the 'evil eye', trying to ward it off with tiny mirrors embroidered into hats and clothing in the south of Pakistan, and extra mirrors on treasured vehicles served thus a dual purpose. More common in the north is the attempt to bind the evil eye with black cloth and thread. A black string around a boy's neck or wrist provides protection from those who look on him with jealousy or envy. Black rags dangling from the mirrors and bumpers of a car or truck keep it out of accidents caused by the evil eye, and protect against theft. It doesn't have much to do with Islam, but then much of what people believe and practise, though they themselves think it to be a part of Islam, are really old, pagan superstitions.

The caste system is the most obvious example. Totally out of keeping with the doctrine of equality between humans which was so central to early Islam, all of Pakistani society is based on it. The most important question involved in choosing a bride for one's son is caste. It is considered a terrible shame to marry into a lower caste. Christians are still treated as unclean because the majority of their ancestors had been 'untouchables', caste-less, so low were they in the social pecking order based on the caste system. That was how the aryan Hindus had subjected the original, highly developed and civilized Dravidian peoples of the subcontinent.

It had hurt to see a Christian shopping in the bazaar. The shopkeeper, a Muslim, would not take payment from the Christian's hand, he had to lay the money on the counter. That way the shopkeeper avoided touching an 'untouchable'. Things were, perhaps, getting better, but it was taking a very long time. There were so many other things too, like Piir worship, the veneration of holy men, miracle workers, 'saints'. The hanging of flags and rags from holy trees to remind God of one's prayers is a relic of ancient Buddhist practice. So many times Muslim activists had defended their theories in the friendly discussions we had by saying that Pakistan was by no stretch of the imagination a Muslim country. Sometimes they meant these phenomena. Other times they meant simply that the vast majority of the people were not committed to living according to the dictates of Islam.

My clothes had dried out and I was already sweating again. I turned my collar inward to keep my kameez-shirt from clinging to the sweat running down my back. My sleeves were wet from the elbows down from wiping the sweat off my brow. I was exhausted. For the last few kilometres the houses had been different, more like city-style

Freedom

bungalows built of burnt brick and surrounded by sour-orange hedges and lower brick walls. Then, in the distance ahead, there were street lanterns. As I walked towards them, still in the middle of the wide wash, the track disappeared and again sand turned to gravel and gravel to stones. All the traffic must have followed another route than the one I was taking.

The wash ended, or so it seemed in the light of the street lanterns to the right and left, in a paved road. I tried to work out where I was. The road might have run from Jamrud to Warsak, where the Canadian government had built a dam on the Kabul river for irrigation and hydroelectric generation. Anyway, that was the general direction the irrigation canal had come from, and there was nowhere else a paved road would want to go.

My feet were hurting. Crossing the street, I sat down on the edge of the road where it fell away to empty my shoes of the sand and gravel that had collected in them. Which way should I go? Going in the direction of Warsak would take me away from Jamrud, but it would be an awful long way to Peshawar that way. On the other hand, I couldn't very well go back towards Jamrud either.

Even though I had only sat for a moment, I already had trouble getting my shoes back on. My feet were swelling. I took my socks off which made just enough difference and I managed to get back into my shoes. I hadn't resolved which way to go yet when something in me pushed me up and straight forward into the darkness. The paved road had acted almost like a dam across the river-bed. On this side of the road the flood-waters had spilled over onto a steeper incline, eroding the earth instead of filling the depressions with sediment as would have been the case where the river-bed had been flat. Again moving away from the light made it that much more difficult to see where I was going. There was a faint glow on the horizon ahead. Only a city would give out enough light to illuminate the sky in such a way. That had to be the outskirts of Peshawar! At least I had a direction to go! There was no path, no bushes, nothing but rock and hard-baked clay.

Low thorn plants caught at the legs of my loose shilwar trousers the first stretch of the way, but soon even they ceased to grow in the hostile, hopelessly eroded environment. The horizon appeared level, but from close up the face of the earth here was a maze of scars and pock-marks. It reflected almost no light. It was impossible here to see where I was going. It was a terrifying feeling, stepping out and waiting for the earth to come up and meet one's step.

I stepped into empty space repeatedly as the level land gave way to gullies washed out by the mountain floods, but to my amazement I always came up standing. I found myself stepping into a gully, skidding and jumping down the rim to keep from falling. 'He will not let your foot slip . . .' Strangely, I could see better down the ravine. It twisted and turned as only the bed of an arbitrary, havoc-wreaking river can. It was no use trying to follow along in the river-bed any more, even though I could see better here: I couldn't see which direction the light on the horizon was, whether the river-bed was leading me toward it or away from it. On the upstream side where I had skidded down, the rim was a slope of maybe forty-five degrees. On the downstream side, where all the force of the water would be pitched against the bank, the bank was perpendicular. I looked for a suitable place only three or four metres high and scaled the opposite side. It was a good thing that I was not going the other way, or I would have fallen off the precipice to the bottom of the ravine. Since I was going in the general down-stream direction, it was the same each time the gulch doubled back across my path: a sudden falling off of the plain into a ditch several metres deep, then a precipice to climb on the other side.

Suddenly the land evened out. It wasn't a natural smoothness, it had to be man-made. A loud whooshing noise and an accompanying breath of wind startled me as something flew within inches of my head. Whatever was dive-bombing me was obviously trying to drive me away from its nest in this hellish desert. A bird might as well make its nest right on the ground amidst the rocks out here, there wouldn't be any predators to speak of. It had to be some sort of rather sizeable bird to make that noise in flying.

As I moved out onto the tarmac I must have walked a sufficient distance from the nest as the buzz-bombing stopped. The tarmac stretched out endlessly. What in the world would anyone want to pave

Freedom

the desert for? Then it dawned on me. It was an airstrip. I had heard about the former American air base at Peshawar in the 1960s. Most of the Christian families had had at least one family member working there – or so it seemed. This landing strip was so huge.[1] It felt strange, almost cumbersome, walking on the perfectly flat, paved surface. After a few minutes I noticed that I had cut across the southern corner of it. I paused to wonder if I should search about for the road that led to the landing field, but thought better of it: it might be at the opposite end of the field, one, maybe even two kilometres away.

The light on the horizon, however, was ahead of me. As I studied the glow in the distance I could distinguish two, perhaps even three separate halos of light merging to one. Was the one distinctly separate glow from the modern suburb of Hyatabad, now under construction, named after Hyatt Sherpao, a former Peshawari Minister in the PPP government of Zulfikar Ali Bhutto and brother of our landlord, who was assassinated by bombing in Lahore in the seventies. Or was it the lights of University Town, where almost all the expatriate population, with the exception of missionaries, lived?

As I drew nearer the glow became fainter and fainter until it disappeared altogether. I had begun to doubt my direction when on the horizon, where the glow had previously served as a beacon to me, two individual lights became visible in the distance. They were no more than an infinitesimal twinkle in the beginning, but gained strength as I approached.

These were the first signs of civilization. I was nearing my goal. Exhaustion made itself felt as I became conscious of the fact that I was really going to make it. I struggled to keep my weary body and tired mind going. If I could only make it to the first settlement. I would go straight to the mosque, the only place a stranger could really go. It was a safe haven. Men often went there to sleep during their lunch break. I would drink my fill, wash my head and feet – I saw the Muslim ritual all of a sudden in a new light – and lie down on a mat and sleep. Sleep!

[1] The police later told me that, in fact, it was not the former American base, which lies on the opposite side of Peshawar, but a secret Pakistan Air Force shooting range, which might also explain some of the craters I encountered en route.

The thought intoxicated me as I stumbled through the sun-baked clay and stone desert. Then, there was no question about it, right in front of me, in the middle of nowhere, were tyre tracks scoring the face of the earth.

Saturday 14th September, 1 a.m.

The tracks led in the general direction of the lights visible ahead, circling around huge pits in the terrain. It looked as if the area had been blanket-bombed, it was so full of craters. Could the immense holes in the face of the earth here have been created by whirlpools during the floods of the monsoon season in July and August of every year? Some were twenty metres across and five, even close to ten metres deep. It looked as if erosion had created subterranean passages between those that were closer together. The water would have to drain off somewhere. Following the tracks of vehicles that had passed through here would keep me from falling into any of the pits.

When was the moon going to come up and provide a little light? It would also be comforting to get my bearings straight, make sure I was walking south and not west, toward the light of Barra in the tribal agency. It dawned on me that the reason I hadn't recognized the formations of the stars as I had studied them from the cave was because I had only had a chance to study the pre-morning sky. If I had only used the chance on Wednesday night more effectively. It must have been about this time that I had woken up to find my guard gone. I had stared at the stars for what had seemed like hours on end, but my mind had been full of the possibilities of escape and weighing the odds. It had only been on the trips down to the cave before sunrise that I had really been able to take a longer look at the constellations. The stars were not in position yet and it would be a matter of hours before they were.

Off to the left, an inky black line on the horizon slowly became discernible against the ultramarine of the midnight sky. What could it be? Did it have something to do with the air strip? Had I unwittingly circled back? Was it barracks or hangars? As I drew closer it became evident that it was much larger than an air base. It continued unbroken for kilometres on end. As I neared the distant line from an angle, I realized that it could only be an endless sea of dwellings forming the perimeter of the desert. Why then the absence of lights? Not one was to be seen in that direction. If there had been electric lights in the areas outlying Jamrud, there certainly should be lights in a place this big!

Then things fell into place: that must be a refugee camp off to the left. It would also explain the multitude of huge craters: the Afghan refugees would have dug mud clay from these spots to build their shelters in this desolate no-man's land. Judging by the unending line on the horizon, there would be mud-quarry craters like these for square kilometres on end. When the refugees had come up against sand or rock at a certain depth, they would have moved on and started a new quarry. Eight to ten years of floods and rains since the refugees had come had made the pits look like the work of erosion.

I would have to try to get around the camp. Refugee camps were off-limits to everyone but the refugees themselves and officials with passes. Foreigners, in particular, were forbidden to enter the camps. The authorities had trouble enough trying to maintain peace among the Afghans living in them, all belonging to various, sometimes warring factions; they didn't want to have to ensure the safety of outsiders.

I continued along the path which slowly became a primitive dirt road. The line of dwellings simply did not end. It was huge, there was absolutely no way I could walk around it.

As if to prove the size of the camp, the road led me into an immense cemetery. Could so many people have died here in the past ten years? Cemeteries were prominent in this part of Pakistan. It was rumoured that the burial ground at Charsadda, continuing for kilometres on end, was one of the largest in the world. It had been growing for centuries. The city had been continually inhabited for over two and a half thousand years: it had been a great city in the time of Alexander the Great. This was only a refugee camp if my guess was right. I wandered through the heaps of stone marking the remains of what must have been thousands of tragedies. Old folk who had just managed to make the rough journey from their homes in the war zones and died here on foreign soil, never to see their fields and homes again. Infants, a scandalous number of pitiful little piles of stones marking an end to a life that had never had a chance. Born to undernourished mothers perhaps, under unsanitary circumstances in the camp, they had died in droves. Young mothers, who had died in childbirth, left alone to cope with their delivery or serviced by unaccustomed and unsterilized hands without proper medical care.

Here in the cemetery was the one place they could be on equal terms with the men that otherwise dominated and restricted their lives. Men, women and children of all ages and walks of life who died of whatever people died of. Their bodies lay a man's height below the earth's surface on a shelf dug into the wall of the grave, its opening covered first by slabs of slate and other rocks, then filled with thorn bushes and packed down with earth, the excess forming a mound a good metre high. Finally, the mound was covered with stones, all as a precaution against jackals and dogs getting into the graves, desecrating the remains. The scrawny, ever hungry pie dogs were ever present, wherever there was a human population.

They soon made themselves noticeable to me. As I drew near the far side of the burial ground and came within earshot of the camp, the barking dogs emerged from between the mounds in a semicircle in front of me. I picked up a few stones – just for sure. They parted to let me pass, closing in behind, snarling, growling and barking. It was rather disconcerting having to watch behind in addition to finding my way ahead. I threw the stones I had in my right hand and bent down to pick up more. The bending down proved to be as effective as chucking the stones itself. It signalled the danger of being hit with stones to the dogs, whereas the ones I had thrown had missed. They backed out of throwing range and eventually lost interest as I left the burial ground and entered the camp. I hadn't noticed how the spread of dwellings had engulfed me also from the right. Trying to circumvent the encampment would mean going back the way I had come and trying to find my way through the endless pits and craters of the desert encompassing it.

Freedom

I pressed onward, compelled by the hopelessness of any other course of action. It was like most Pakistani slum areas, the houses hidden behind the mud walls providing shelter from the eye of the public. The doors in the walls were often invisible behind a curtain that maintained the required privacy even when the door was opened. Nothing was left to chance in maintaining *purdah*, the seclusion of women, even though it would be put down to fate if it failed. Women and fate didn't mix. If someone glimpsed your womenfolk, it was the women's fault. Not that any flesh would be exposed even behind the 'curtain' but seeing a woman's uncovered head, a female face, the opportunity to communicate through a smile, a twinkle in the eye, that look . . . was enough to put a husband, brother or father in a blind rage.

Perhaps they had reason to doubt the intentions of their women. A Muslim friend of mine, an educated and well-to-do business man, had once told me that he would never let his wife go out of the house unaccompanied by his driver or night watchman. Not because he was worried someone else would take advantage of her, but because you couldn't trust a woman when it came to sex. They were inherently promiscuous, always waiting for their chance. Given just the slightest opportunity they would prove unfaithful. I had asked him if he didn't trust his own wife. 'Of course not!' he had answered. Judging by the exploits his customers had bragged about when I had been in his shop once, thinking I didn't understand the vernacular, he just might have been right. Sex was in the air. The repression of it forced it to the surface in the most unlikely way. On the bus men studied the shoes of women covered completely by *burqa*. If a hand was visible their eyes would be riveted to it, judging by the complexion and shape of the fingers what the rest of the body would be like, letting their imagination carry away. Who needed to see a beautiful or sexy woman when you could imagine her, naked, right there in front of you on the bus?

Those women who didn't wear the *burqa*, the 'shuttlecock', or 'tent', as it was referred to with ridicule by some, wore the *chadar*, a large sheet or blanket wrapped around head and shoulders. Some left their faces bare, others covered all but their eyes. Those were the worst, often shameless in their staring. One of the better-looking of my male missionary colleagues had said that he had felt as if he had been eaten alive by some of these women, who from the anonymity of their chadars devoured him with their eyes. Even those who were not so shameless communicated sexuality through their coy demureness, allowing eye contact for only a split second, then casting their eyes to the ground.

Now, however, the world within these walls was closed by a further shroud of silence and darkness. The silence of the sleeping camp made me wonder whether it was empty. No, climbing the track that was slowly becoming something like a street further from the perimeter, the odd sign of life became audible. On the left, in a house a baby was crying.

What if one of these families, wakened by a child, heard me scurrying past and someone got up to see what was happening? How would I explain to these Pushto and Dari speakers what I was doing in the camp at this time of night? On the right a dog barked at my approach. That was potentially even more dangerous. I hissed at it *chup! hadd!* hoping that these Urdu language commands were similar in either Persian or the language of the Pathans and threw a few stones to make sure my message got across. A yelp and a quick exit on the part of the dog told of a hit. When was I going to get out of this maze of mud dwellings? They seemed to have no end. The light ahead now had to be some part of Peshawar, it was so bright on the horizon.

A loud snoring on the right made me cringe. I strained to see in the midnight shadows as I moved on without slackening pace. The dim outline of a charpai in a doorway was barely discernible. An elderly man, perhaps aroused by his own snoring, turned over and the snoring stopped. Which way had he turned, towards me or away from me? Was he silent because he was watching me or had the snoring stopped just because he had changed positions? I held my breath and wondered if my heart had stopped. The seconds dragged on as I moved ahead, driven by instinct or another subconscious force. There was no shout, no question. The pounding in my chest resumed and reassured me that my heart had not stopped. Having passed the one, the second and the third along the route were not as alarming. Here, in the midst of the camp there were more men sleeping in the street outside their houses, probably trying to catch whatever little of the nightly desert breeze might make it that far through the maze of high-walled dwellings. On the right, where one of the myriad of narrow alley-like lanes threading haphazardly through the sea of mud walls provided me with the ever present choice of which way to turn, there was a more permanent-looking house with steel gate and a high-backed lorry standing behind it outlined in the light of a bare bulb hanging from a pole. Electricity! The bright light lay still ahead, but I felt that my goal was getting nearer. The camp would certainly merge into the city in the next few blocks.

I was wrong. The kilometres seemed endless. What kind of madness was this? There just couldn't be so many houses in a refugee camp. Was I running around in circles? No, the light on the horizon was still straight ahead beyond the black of the buildings. Then, as the street straightened out, a massive floodlight on top of a high pole spilled its glaring bright white luminescence on the path before me. As I drew nearer the object the pool of light was focused on became visible. Whitewashed buildings surrounded by a high, barbed-wire fence. Was it a prison for detainees? Illegal refugees? For those who rioted or brought the battle across the border in Afghanistan into the camp? Before I could get a closer look at the buildings to determine what they were I noticed a movement directly between me and the barbed-wire enclosure. I quickly shifted the bundle of my own clothes onto my left shoulder to cover my white face. It would look like a rolled-up chadar, the way many men carried theirs, nothing out of the ordinary. Over the top of it I followed out of the corner of my eye as a man, obviously a night watchman, raised himself on his elbow and looked at me as I passed. Again my heart skipped a beat as I waited for the inevitable 'who goes there?' but he didn't say anything, just let himself back down on his mat, letting me pass unchallenged. What did he think? Wasn't it worth the hassle getting into an argument with a proud, angry Afghan about his movements? One didn't challenge these people lightly.

Escape from terror

Passing through the bright lights of the huge barbed-wire enclosure, I was blinded to anything beyond the circle of light. I couldn't see the road ahead in the darkness, and at my feet the street had vanished into a waste of hard-baked hoof- and foot-marked mud that had preserved the footprints since the puddle from the last rains had dried up. The mud spread out in all directions. Which way was the road? I felt the watchman's eyes in my back, had to keep going, had to keep going in the right direction. Was the road to the left of the pole holding the light or to the right? Somewhere in the distance to the left the other light I had seen from far off was visible for a moment. These were the beacons that had beckoned me and guided me through the last stretch of desert and the camp up to here. But where to from here? I had to find a continuation of the road.

Ahead, all was blackness. Above all else, I had to get out of the watchman's sight. I held to the right of the lamp-post. An office building loomed up from the shadows as I passed the light, getting it behind me and out of my eyes. The road, or at least a road, was right there! Where it would take me, I had no idea. At least it would be away from the desert, and, as it was a proper gravel road, it had to lead somewhere, somewhere the people went to and came from. It had to lead me to Peshawar, where else would the traffic go? With the light behind me I could make out enough of the buildings to notice that this was not a residential area, at least not like the mass of mud homes I had come through. These were better built buildings, more like the burnt-brick buildings typical of the city. Maybe I was coming to the city now. The better road seemed to indicate that. Ahead, all was darkness.

Then I saw the mosque I had been waiting for to my right, set back a little from the road. Though made of mud, unlike the last buildings I had seen since passing the guard and the lighted, barbed-wire enclosure, it was clearly a mosque; the minaret for the call to prayer and the *mithrab* bay in one wall denoted the *qibla*, or direction of Mecca, and facilitating prayers established that beyond a doubt. My exhaustion propelled me toward it, the one thought of rest filling my mind. As I neared the mosque I felt a growing sense of fear and repulsion. There was something spooky about the place that I couldn't explain. I had always enjoyed going to see mosques of historic importance and architectural beauty, some of those in Pakistan unsurpassed by any structure as examples of artistic construction and masons' craftsmanship. There was something wrong with this place, something bad about it. I couldn't explain it to myself. Some people claimed visiting any mosque brought a spiritual battle and possible spiritual oppression. I had never felt that way as I regarded such superstition a negation of the supremacy of Christ. I was willing to make an exception in this case and gave up my plan of getting some rest, the atmosphere not in the least conducive to it. It would be no good waking up in a refugee camp with the men coming for morning prayers anyway. I moved on.

A few hundred metres down the road an odd rushing of the wind caught my attention. I couldn't feel any significant breeze, where was the noise coming from? Ahead and to the right a skeleton of a building appeared. It was a high, steel frame structure, high enough to obstruct winds that had not found their way down to where thousands upon thousands of refugees and I sweated in the night heat. Then it struck me that I knew what I was looking at. That very instant I also registered the fear that had been creeping up on me since I had approached the mosque. I recognized the looming, howling skeleton. It was the ruins of the 'Shelter Now International' workshop, which had been plundered and burnt some months ago by radical fundamentalists in the camp, that was groaning in the wind. This was the infamous Nasir Bagh Camp[2] that I had wandered into!

I remembered the day vividly when I had dropped by the SNI offices and had a press release packet pressed into my hand. That was where I had seen this skeleton of a structure before, in the high-gloss black-and-white photographs contained in the packet. SNI had been doing highly valued work in the camps providing, among other things, more durable types of dwellings and vocational training, also

[2]In fact it was one of six individual camps clustered over an area of several square kilometres, each designed to house 30,000 refugees, but, as the Deputy Inspector General, Police told me later, in fact contained more like 60,000 persons each, making for a total population in Nasir Bagh of 360,000 displaced persons.

for women. The latter had angered the fundamentalists in the camp, so on the big *Eid* holiday, when thousands of men were gathered for *Juma* prayers, the mullah, or main Muslim cleric of the mosque had agitated the crowd in his sermon, instigating them to riot against the foreigners who 'ruined their women'. The mob had stolen the vehicles and pilfered the workshop, destroying and burning whatever they had no use for or could not be taken along.

The goose-pimples chased up and down my back. I wanted to get out of here. This was one place I couldn't afford to be detected. I pressed onward past the charred frame, moving as quickly as I could short of outright running. My fear left no room for the exhaustion I had begun to succumb to. After a short while the buildings began to thin out. Someone was snoring on what seemed to be the veranda of a bazaar. I heard a voice across the road on the left: were there people talking, was it a radio, or was it someone mumbling in his sleep? Someone was walking along the road, the sound of stones being scattered was unmistakable. Should I stop and wait for him to pass? I didn't have the nerve. Besides, that would mean I didn't want to be seen, had something to hide. It would arouse suspicion. What if the people in the shadows of the verandas were following my movements already, thinking me to be one of them? I couldn't stop, I had to go on. As I drew closer to the sound of steps on the gravel road, they suddenly became erratic as they made room for me. A stifled bray told me it was a donkey I had scared off the road, where it had probably been dozing on its feet. I breathed a sigh of relief. It was only an animal. Donkeys tried to keep out of reach of people, they were so used to being beaten with rods by their handlers. My relief grew as I emerged from the bazaar and found myself in open country again. I was out of danger here. All I needed to do was concentrate on maintaining my pace, hoping that this road would lead me sooner or later to the safety of the city.

On the left I saw the silhouette of a large sign. I went right up to it to see if it bore any information relevant to my whereabouts. I couldn't see any writing on it even though I put my nose right up to it in the darkness, hoping to find some faint traces of text on the rusty

Freedom

sheet of tin. Then something made me circle round the other side of it. There was definitely writing on it – English! Pressing my face right up to it again I could just make it out in the darkness:

> DANGER! YOU ARE NOW ENTERING NASIR BAGH
> CAMP NO. 2. NO UNAUTHORIZED PERSONS
> BEYOND THIS POINT. OFF LIMITS TO
> FOREIGNERS WITHOUT WRITTEN PERMISSION OF
> THE DEPUTY COMMISSIONER FOR REFUGEES.

I was terribly relieved to be on the other side of that sign now! I had just walked clean through Nasir Bagh 2 . . . What would the authorities have done if they had caught me in there? Supposed me to be a spy? Peshawar was full of spies. It was fabled to be a richer intelligence pantry than Vienna or Berlin in the days of the cold war. If I had been picked up here there would have been any number of reasons to suspect me of being an insurgent or agent, perhaps even more likely, a drug dealer. With Islamabad cracking down on poppy cultivation in the tribal area I had just left, Afghanistan was more than making up for the deficit in heroin production. The newspaper articles were mind-boggling with their reports of seizures of heroin being transported down-country by the ton. In Europe or the USA a kilogram of powder was big time. This was the source. Jamrud and Barra brokered most of the Afghanistan output. Rumours persisted that people in high places actually managed the illicit trade including a former governor of the NWF Province.[3]

Foreigners ending up in jail in Peshawar did so because they were involved in the drug trade. One American recently arrested at Peshawar airport had concealed an egg filled with heroin in his rectum. He had obviously been set up or ratted on . . . I was truly relieved to be out of the camp and out of the forbidden area. On the other hand, the precariousness of my situation became more clear to me on reading the sign. Even being near this area could be interpreted

[3]He was subsequently ambushed and assassinated in a professionally executed hit not far from our home.

as bad intent. What would a foreigner be doing this time of night on foot and alone at the entrance to a refugee camp if not making mischief? Would anyone believe my story as it had really happened? Or would it just be taken for a tall tale dreamed up to get me off the hook? Would my disappearance be taken for a ruse to throw a smoke-screen over covert activities?[4]

Further on there were scattered buildings again, but more perplex-ing to me was a new rushing sound, different from the wind chasing through the ribs of the gutted SNI structure. As I drew closer it became more intense. Could it be that there was a waterfall in the vicinity? I couldn't imagine that. Maybe there were rapids. That would be more likely. The Kabul river must lie ahead. Had I veered off so far to the north-east? I had guessed I was going in the general direction of University Town, almost due south of Jamrud. Or was it a tube-well pumping station, pumping water from the water table a hundred metres below the surface into a gathering pool feeding irrigation ditches? That might be it. I was coming into the fertile, irrigated reaches of the Peshawar valley, the fruit basket of Pakistan, but I hadn't reached the city yet. There was no sign of it anymore, not even a brightness on the horizon. How long would I be able to keep going? Weakness and exhaustion harried the angels keeping me on my feet.

As the din of rushing water grew I passed out of the shadow of a building and saw the whitewashed booth perched like a lighthouse on a small bridge spanning a large canal, a single bulb dangling from a wire sending light to the checkpoint. The sound of falling water had its source here where water was gushing over a distribution sluice in the canal. The roaring of the water drowned out the noise of my movements to my own ears. I would have to cross that bridge where the checkpoint was if I was to keep going in the same direction I had been following. A chain was strung across the bridge at the booth. Was it meant to keep people in, or out? At this time of night, probably both, I thought. Coming closer, I saw that there was no alternative to

[4] Later such allegations were in fact levelled at me by a party in the church that was trying to get their own candidate elected as bishop. Others blamed them for setting up my kidnapping. Neither was true.

my crossing the bridge and passing the picket. On the left was a tent, presumably where the guard slept when off-duty. On the right there was only a narrow path leading to some shacks on the bank of the canal. Swimming across further downstream would be refreshing, but there were lighted bazaar booths lining the other side in that direction and, from the look of it, I wouldn't get very far down my side along the little path that was crowded out by the mud walls of dwellings built on the bank of the canal.

The checkpoint looked empty. Nothing was to be seen behind the chest-high walls that were probably meant to provide a measure of firing cover, if there were to be any shoot out. I would have to take the chance. Without slackening pace, I pressed on past. Looking sideways through the door as I drew abreast, I forgot about the chain I had registered, almost tripping over it. The police officer on duty was sitting on the floor of the booth. In my momentum, I barely cleared the chain with my right foot after coming up against it with my left shin, probably rattling it and coming down hard on my foot as I tried to catch myself. He started. Grabbing his carbine he sprang to his feet and switched off the light, which blinded him to my movements in the shadows not more than ten metres away. Before his eyes adjusted to the darkness I was across the canal. I had to make another snap decision at the end of the bridge. It was a T-junction. If I turned right, I would walk right in front of the lighted bazaar booths. To the left there was only inky blackness.

That was what I needed, cover. As I stepped off the bridge and passed a small date palm, I drew a breath again. From the cover of the shadows I could just see the guard scanning the road in all three directions. He hadn't seen me moving, only heard an unaccustomed noise over the din of the waterfall he had grown used to. He searched the darkness for a moment longer before stepping out of the picket booth and ducking into his tent. Was he waking someone up for the next watch? It seemed I had just made it in time before lights out. How would I have negotiated the situation in the dark? What would have happened if the guard's eyes had been accustomed to the dark? I didn't like to think about it.

Escape from terror

I was walking on asphalt now, one step closer to civilization. My legs were cramping up and my feet aching. Walking on the hard, flat surface was unbearable. I hadn't emptied my shoes for ages, hadn't wanted to break the rhythm that kept me moving ahead. Pulling off my shoes, I realized it wasn't gravel that had been bothering my feet, but blisters. I had to break them in order to keep going. The large flaps of loose skin I tore off. If they were going to get infected, it would have happened already. Anyway, who cared about that? The main thing was to make it home? If I could only find the strength to keep going. Or should I lie down till morning? I was out of tribal territory now, past the police post controlling access to the camps.

I followed the canal upstream, going towards the Warsak Dam, which meant also towards Warsak Road. Somewhere along the way there would be a road or trail cutting off to the right, saving me the extra distance of walking all the way to the dam. I would run into Warsak Road sooner or later and could then follow it in to where we lived in the Cantonment. If I were to lie down I would be so stiff by morning that I wouldn't be able to get up. It was better to keep moving, like a machine, always the same rhythm, same speed.

It seemed the road would never end. I must have walked along the canal for the better part of an hour, passing an underground aquaduct where the whole canal disappeared beneath a dry river-bed, only to pop up boiling in the vertical shaft spilling into the groove of the embankment rising above the plain on the other side. From there it carried the precious commodity tens of kilometres to fields and orchards that would otherwise be desert. For a long way the lower ground to the right was a waterlogged jumble of scrub trees and swamp grass. As the ground rose to meet the level of the canal there were buildings, probably housing maintenance units for the canal. They were not surrounded by enclosing walls, so they weren't homes. Here and there a light bulb accented a structure. Some of them looked like small factories with their tin roofs and iron-barred windows. I must be getting closer to the Warsak Dam Road. On the left, the far side of the canal, there were dwellings bunched together at irregular intervals. Were they further refugee camps or just poor villages? The villagers in this part of the country weren't a whole lot better off than the refugees. As I plodded past, here and there a rooster arched itself and drummed its wings against its breast. It wasn't time to crow yet, though.

Saturday, 2 a.m.

'Who goes there?' In the dark I hadn't seen the road-block.

'It's just me,' I replied without thinking about it, startled into speech by a human voice, uninhibited by the naivety of my answer.

Had I been addressed in Pushto or Urdu? I couldn't say. Cautiously I approached, making out the road-block just a few steps before reaching it. A boom was lowered across the road and several men in shilwar-kameez uniform were standing behind it next to the charpais they had been sitting or lying on until they had heard me coming and challenged me. I ducked under the barrier and headed straight for the nearest charpai, so tired and aching all I could think of was sitting while they interrogated me.

'Kahan ja rayah ho?' They had at least gathered that I had spoken to them in Urdu and were complying, asking me where I was going.

'Pikhawar,' I replied, this time using the local Pushto pronunciation of the city's name.

One of them took my bundle of clothes and checked to see if it contained anything suspicious. For some reason he didn't notice anything strange about the clothes, their being western. Maybe it was due to the darkness.

'Wapas jana!' he commanded. 'Pikhawar us taraf hai.'

I thought he was just saying it to get me to turn back from the road-block, telling me to go back, that Peshawar lay in the opposite direction.

'But I have to get home before morning. I want to go in on Warsak Road,' I argued, having learned from almost five years in Pakistan that arguing with officials and police was a way of life, almost a requirement. Nobody in their right mind simply gave in the first time they heard 'no' for an answer. Missionary wives had a hard time accepting it when their husbands adopted the local custom.

'No-one is allowed beyond this point.'

'But I have to go home!'

'Go back where you came from!'

'You mean I have to go all the way back past Nasir Bagh?'

'There's another police post a few kilometres past it, they'll tell you the way.'

'Pani to dena,' I demanded, determined not to budge from the charpai I was sitting on until they had given me water to drink. One of the men dug an old gallon oil can from under the string bed and gave it to me. The water tasted better than I had drunk in the cave, even though I was drinking from a rusty tin can with rough edges. I hoped the water wasn't taken straight from the open canal. I drank my fill and rose to go, feeling the strain on the cramped muscles throughout my body already beginning to stiffen up with my motionlessness.

I guessed they had taken me for a lunatic, wandering around at this time of night with no sense of direction. My appearance would have only corroborated the evidence and cinched the verdict. I could only be glad they hadn't taken me for some hard-up drug addict who had robbed a foreigner and stolen his clothes. That they hadn't expected anything out of the ordinary was a total surprise to me. How was it possible that they could take me for a local?

I didn't have the energy to think about it. My mind was filled with the realization that I had walked an hour for nothing and would have to walk another, just to get back to Nasir Bagh camp. What if what they had told me was not true, that this road did not lead to Peshawar? Even if it did, would I get past the post at Nasir Bagh a second time? This time I would have to walk through the lighted bazaar area. They had said there was another road-block ahead of that. The hour's walk seemed endless. About half-way back another pack of dogs raised a ruckus as I approached. I stooped to pick up some rocks. The road was asphalt! I went over to the canal bank and dug four or five medium-sized stones out of the clay, clenching them in my fist. The dogs backed away and eventually lost interest in me. The canal was full: it must have still been full from the monsoon rains and the melting snow of the Hindu Kush Range towering above Kabul.

I lay down on the cement wall retaining the canal water at the spot where the water disappeared down a vertical shaft, to cross underneath the dry river-bed, and wet my head. It helped a bit, but didn't return any of the strength I had expended. I couldn't think of when I had ever been so physically tired. Even the time I had got lost jogging in Rome and ended up running fifteen kilometres over a period of an hour and a half before I made it back to the hotel for breakfast hadn't been this wearying. Although each muscle, joint, ligament and tendon in my body was crying out in pain at having been so maltreated by my inconsideration of what they could bear, they were also jubilant at having the weight off my feet. I'd never realized that pain could feel so wonderful. I'd been walking since about 9 p.m., and for several kilometres from the cave to the chieftain before that. Had I walked thirty kilometres, or even thirty-five, sitting only very briefly twice till now? By any standard it was enough for one day. Perhaps I should just stay right here for the rest of the night! All the good reasons for not going any further began to fill my mind. It would scare my family to death if I woke them knocking on the door at this time of night. In the morning someone would walk by and I could ask which really was the shortest way to Peshawar. Who was to know, perhaps the road-block was only effective after curfew. Why waste time and strength going back where I had come from, even if it was only a few more kilometres to Nasir Bagh.

The moon was just rising. It seemed crazy, but I had the instinctive feeling that I had to keep going. I had to force myself to get up and move on, the stiffness already getting so bad that I was afraid I wouldn't be able to take one step more. I dragged myself onto my knees and felt an enormous weight pinning me down as I struggled to my feet. I decided not to stop any more, no matter how tired I was, until I got home or to some form of conveyance.

Saturday, 3 a.m.

The lights were off and there was no-one in the booth at the Nasir Bagh camp bridge. By the light of the moon I could see quite plainly across the canal and did not detect anyone on guard duty. Maybe the two-hour detour had been worthwhile after all. Straight ahead the lights were still on in the bazaar, but now there was no guard looking for my silhouette in them. My spirits rose as I walked past the bridge unchallenged. Even if someone did see me now I was outside the camp and passing it on a public thoroughfare. What would be strange about that? I was now a free man on free soil, I imagined. Least of all would the guard suspect me of being the one who had sneaked out of the camp. No-one would be crazy enough to double back after getting past unscathed once. The canal was on the right, with the checkpoint and chain at the far end of the bridge. The moon had climbed an hour's journey above the Hindu Kush mountain range in the distant north-east, and with the light switched off the visibility was good. 'Thank you, God, that you took care of the timing,' I breathed, conscious of the fact that although I had walked five to ten kilometres extra it had not been futile. Things could have turned nasty if I had been apprehended coming out.

On the left I passed the bazaar. It seemed to be mostly tea stalls, 'hotels' and the odd firewood merchant with the obligatory tobacco and soft drink kiosks in-between. In the 'hotels', groups of string beds under a canopy of canvas and reed matting supported by the irregular trunks of forearm-thick saplings, the kitchen utensils were all packed away for the night, leaving the mud combination stoves/counters bare. A few men lay asleep on charpais wrapped up in thin sheets, more to protect against mosquitos than chill, I guessed, as it was still unbearably hot. If this had been the city, and electricity more reliable, those men would all be sleeping under a pedestal fan going full blast. That killed two birds with one stone: it kept the mosquitos off and kept one cool enough for sleep as well. Those who could, would carry their string beds and pedestal fans up onto the roof of their home, where it would be coolest, away from the heat trapped inside the walls the sun had beaten on so mercilessly all day.

Freedom

I had walked through unpopulated wilderness with young eucalyptus, *pipal*, *neem*, and a variety of other trees thriving off the seepage from the canal on the other side of the road and wondered whether this really could be the right direction, when the road turned left. That brought me back closer to the course I had planned. I was going south again. Going the other way I had hoped to come into the city from the north along Warsak Road. This route would have to bring me in from the west via University Town. I had no idea that the Nasir Bagh Camps were so far from the metropolis. Maybe this was the shortest way after all.

A light became visible in the distance. It turned out to be just a few kilometres from the bazaar to the police station. The picket post outside the fortified station was unmanned and the steel door to the station was locked. The place reminded me somehow of a medieval castle, if less romantic than the new red brick ones the police were building throughout the province at strategic points along the major thoroughfares. They looked like something out of the world of Disney, although they were most certainly not meant to be decorative as much as to provide protection from angry mobs. Medieval castles with their towers, high walls and brickwork balustrades weren't meant to look romantic either. Romanticism interpreted the past from a totally different reality, one where life had lost its cutting edge, its intensity, its danger, its tenacity. After slowing for just a moment to think whether I should knock on the door and ask for help, I pushed past the post, thinking it would be quicker and simpler if I could just get home without having to deal with the police. About a kilometre down the road, however, the road-block was manned.

Bright lighting at the barrier heralded it in good time. I tried to judge the terrain on both sides. There was an artificial embankment on the right. That would be the raised bank of a canal. It was no use trying to circle that way. On the left there was 'jungle', in the original Indian subcontinent sense: scrub, elephant grass, twisted trees and brush, not the lush green mammoth trees encircled by creepers and vines as I had grown up to understand the word. There would be lots of cover that way, but was it worth it trying? There were rifle-toting police milling about and anyway, I didn't have anything to hide. If things went as well as at the previous road block, I would just talk my way through.

A Bible verse I had learned as a child came to mind: 'Trust in the Lord with all your heart and lean not on your own understanding. In all your ways acknowledge him, and he will direct your paths . . .' He had taken good care of me until now, why shouldn't I trust him here too? Come to think of it, he had never let me down yet, although things often turned out differently from what I had expected or even asked, and weren't by any means always easy solutions while they lasted. That was the key, while they lasted. They were sometimes terrible while they lasted, just like this. It wasn't until afterwards that things usually made sense. At least they fitted together in such a way as to give meaning to life and lead to life situations I would not have wanted to have missed.

Besides, I was so at the end of my strength that I couldn't imagine trying to pick my way silently through the bush. I stuck to the middle of the road and plodded on towards the road-block. I would just have to see what happened.

'Assalamo-aleikum,' I called out to the wisp of a man standing guard when I had come far enough out of the shadows for him to glance up at having noticed my movement.

'U-aleikum-assalam!' He replied cheerfully, returning my greeting as if my coming was, if not expected, the most natural thing in the world. Again the same question: where I was going? The same answer: home.

As I approached the barrier his eye travelled over me in either a practised or intelligent way and he noticed something about my bundle of clothes, also my clenched fist.

'What have you got in your hand?' he asked.

I hadn't noticed that I was still carrying the stones. I opened my fist and showed him the rocks on the flat of my palm I had dug from the bank of the canal.

'What are they for?'

'The dogs.'

He laughed in an approving sort of way. There was something

about him that I liked, that disarmed me of my reservations and fears. He didn't appear to be a threat or a problem. Even when he asked next for my papers, it wasn't threatening: it was normal to have to produce one's identity card or refugee identification. How else were they to establish who was lawfully in the country and who not?

'I don't have any,' I replied, knowing that would never be a satisfactory answer.

'Why don't you have any, where are you coming from?' he asked, at once alert as I stopped at the barrier. It sounded almost more like a pleasantry than interrogation the way he asked it, although I was sure he was doing his job, not making small talk.

'It's a long story, I'm not sure you'll want to hear it,' I procrastinated.

'Why shouldn't I? Try me!'

'It's not that easy to explain, you'd need a lot of time . . .'

'I've got all the time in the world!' he replied, giving vent to the boredom of his job on the night shift.

He led me around the barrier and motioned for me to 'sit', at the same time taking my bundle from me as his less bright colleagues had an hour or so before.

This constable was brighter, unrolling my bundle of clothing he recognized that it was 'British'. Or was it just that the light was brighter, revealing that it was a shirt with clerical collar and linen trousers with belt and buckle I had rolled up, not the generously cut shilwar trousers with their two-metre waist and the knee-length kameez shirt. Even the dimmest of wits would have to see that in the bright light of this checkpoint.

'Yeh to British hain . . .' he commented under his breath with no little wonderment.

'What is your name?' he asked, coming back to protocol.

'Paul Murdoch,' I replied, matter-of-fact. He didn't seem to hear, at least he didn't react in any way to the name.

'Why are you carrying these English clothes?' he continued, speaking all the while in Urdu, and with just a tinge of reprimand or accusation in his voice.

'They are mine.'

'Are you a foreigner then?' he asked, surprised, only then perhaps noticing my skin colour as unusually light even for an Afghan or Pathan.

'Ba-ilqul,' by all means, I asserted. In my exhausted state it never dawned on me that in my condition it would be difficult for anyone to believe I was a foreigner.

He hurried to offer me a chair, obviously 'knowing' that foreigners couldn't, or was it shouldn't, squat . . .

'I have lots of foreigner friends,' he told me enthusiastically. 'They always wave to me when they drive past into the camps for work. There are doctors, teachers, all kinds of good people.'

The kind of good people the fundamentalists had instigated the refugees to riot against, I thought, keeping my counsel. That was one of the things the less fortunate among the Pakistanis appreciated about foreigners: usually they treated one as an equal. A French doctor or a German engineer going into the camp would consider it quite normal to greet this unassuming, lowly son of a poor family as a fellow human being, maybe even exchange a few words with him. Mind you, they wouldn't necessarily do it back home in France or Germany if he were there as a guest worker; that was another matter altogether. Treating everyone as equals in this country wasn't easy though, for many reasons. For one, it created conflicts in one's relationships with other classes and castes. Acquaintances who were better situated in society had sometimes crossed the street to avoid meeting me if I was with a sweeper or someone of the servant class. Other, more open-minded friends had sometimes asked why in the world I would want to associate with such people. Sometimes I felt as if I was being forced to choose between classes.

As a Christian and a missionary, I had once even been forced into officially stating that my solidarity was with the poor and the oppressed. It was difficult for other reasons too. Accepting people as equals made one also vulnerable. Perhaps that was why it was so tightly guarded against in this society. More than once I had been taken advantage of. It was as if by respecting someone lower than yourself on the social ladder you automatically lost their respect. But what if it wasn't really respect that one lost, but a servile fear, a grudging recognition that one had the means to coerce obedience and a kind of wallowing subservience that I had found disgusting. In that case, one hadn't lost anything at all. Respect, real respect had to be earned any way you looked at it. That was the only meaningful respect there was on offer. I wondered if that were understood in the West any better than here.

'But you don't work in the camp, do you?' He was talking to me. 'I haven't ever seen you drive past!'

'No, I've never been here before!'

'But what are you doing here now?' he asked, truly interested and excited at the prospect of forging a friendship with a foreigner.

'Like I said, it's a long story . . .'

'Go ahead and tell it!' he implored me, squatting down at my side, dropping protocol where he had picked it up.

'Well,' I started out, 'a week ago I was kidnapped by . . .'

Before I could finish the sentence he had jumped up and blurted out:

'You must be Doctor Paul!'

'Yes,' I replied (that was what everybody called me, that or 'Paal-seb' if it was just a fleeting Pathan acquaintance), totally confused that he should know my name but not have recognized it when I told him it just a minute before.

'I know all about you!' he cried. 'I have your car's registration number here somewhere in the journal!'

In his excitement he grabbed the journal from a small, rickety table and began frantically leafing through it backwards and forwards looking for the entry concerning my disappearance. He was so flustered he couldn't locate it, but asserted repeatedly that it was in there somewhere and he knew all about it. I wondered if he was illiterate, like three out of four in this country.

'Just think of it!' he exulted, giving up on the journal and placing it back on the table. 'I found the missing foreigner! Remember to put in a good word for me, maybe I'll get a promotion!'

I assured him I would do whatever I could.

'They didn't beat you, did they?' he asked with a note of true concern, returning from his self-congratulatory mood to my plight, and at the same time releasing me from the necessity of telling him the whole story.

'Not after the actual kidnapping.'

'That's good,' he sighed his relief for me.

I really could have been treated worse I thought to myself. Look at the bright side. It was over now and could have been worse. It really could have got ugly when the two ringleaders were killed.

'Do you know what happened to the two who got killed?' I was interested in knowing the actual facts. He hadn't heard anything. I wondered what had really happened.

'But you must be hungry!' he said.

'Actually I'm more thirsty,' I said, asking for water.

'You will have water, tea, bread, food, cigarettes, everything you want, you are my guest!' he stated with that grandiose abandon that only a Pakistani man knew.

He called a lesser constable doing chores outside a small thatch shelter to bring water. I drank glass after glass from the tall aluminium, deformed beaker, which he refilled from a plastic canister. These boys were definitely better off, or at least more cultured than the ones I had met further up the canal.

He asked the constable to see if there was food left to offer me.

'Ji han,' was the reply in the affirmative and he promised to bring it at once.

He arrived shortly and unwrapped a bold block-printed cotton cloth that held a *roti*, or *naan*, the flat bread eaten with curries and being the staple, used as a synonym for food in general. 'Our daily bread . . .' Pakistani Christians understood that in precisely the way Jesus had meant it when he taught his disciples to pray.

'I guess the curry is finished . . .?' he asked the other sheepishly, embarrassed that he couldn't offer me any with the bread. 'Bring a tomato then,' he ordered.

'Sorry sir, there aren't any tomatoes left either,' was the depressing reply. 'I'll see if there is an onion,' he said and walked off to the hut. In a while he was back with a small onion peeled with a pocket knife and cut into crescent-like slivers. He placed them in a small dish used to hold the sauce-like curry and handed it to me apologetically.

I ate about half the bread with some onion slivers, and they brought tea. That was good. Small cups of hot, sweet tea. Again they apologized for not having any milk to go in it.

'I'll get you a ride into town to your home with the patrol car when it comes by, you'll be home in no time!' he promised as I drank my tea.

Car lights approached almost at a walking pace from the direction of Peshawar, and my 'host' went down towards the gate to do his duty. It was a police pickup on patrol duty with a load of sepoys in the back. He tried to stop them before they reached the barrier, talking to them through the cab window as he walked alongside, but they hardly slowed for him, flashing their headlights to the constable on the gate to raise it, leaving my intercessor standing with outstretched arms to curse his luck, or them, or both. There went my ride, I thought. The tall, skinny policeman came back and remonstrated about the pickup not stopping.

'Come on, I'd better take you to my officer,' he said, seeing that I had finished with my meal. He led me up the embankment of the canal onto its rim. At a sluice gate the officer in charge was asleep on a string bed. Actually he was not asleep, 'stupor' would fit his condition better. The policeman saluted with deference and explained the situation to him.

'You want a smoke?' he asked, being friendly enough as he rose onto his elbow from his doze. I declined, saying that I had already been offered a cigarette.

'But we've got bharay-huay "filled" cigarettes,' he tried to entice me.

'What do you mean with "bharay-huay", "filled" with what?' I asked, always eager to learn new expressions in Urdu. I guessed that 'loaded' would fit the idiom better than 'filled'.

'Hashish,' he replied, quite matter of fact, adding that they had everything a fellow could dream of at this police post.

So that was what they did with the drugs confiscated from smugglers bringing it out of the tribal territory, where it was sold on the street quite openly, I thought to myself.

'No thanks, I don't use *nashah*,' I said, declining his offer of drugs.

'Take him to the post and give him a bed for the rest of the night, and report to the SHO (Senior Head Officer),' he reminded my host.

Saturday, 4 a.m.

We walked the kilometre back to the fort-like police station where the policeman banged on the steel door until he woke the duty officer who woke a junior sepoy to open the door. The officer on duty sitting behind the desk with a telephone was a normal, uneducated man who couldn't decide what to do: wake the SHO and incur his wrath for waking him at four in the morning or let him sleep and incur his wrath for not reporting immediately?

The police station was a cloister of rooms around a veranda that circled a courtyard with a water spicket and a few trees. The man on duty sat behind a small table serving as a desk on the veranda, where it would be a bit cooler than in the rooms.

'Can I call my home?' I asked, seeing the telephone on the night watch's desk. 'They will be worried about me.'

'The hand-set with dialling facility is in the SHO's room,' he explained, 'this one only receives calls.'

He banged on his hand-set anyway, pulled on the jerried telephone wire with its bared ends that had been strung up for this makeshift extension and asked the phone number I wanted, trying it, as if by some miracle the phone might work anyway. After a couple of fruitless attempts he gave up, shrugging at me, saying no-one else had access to the outgoing line except the commanding officer, who kept the main extension with him in his room. I guessed he didn't trust his subordinates with the phone. They might call everyone and his uncle, blocking the line for incoming calls besides running up a bill.

The man who had brought me in pressed him to wake the SHO,

but to no avail. My copper was obviously pretty low on the pecking order. In the end they reached a compromise: they woke the Assistant Head Officer, who appeared sleep-drunk in the doorway, holding himself up by the door-frame and told them to give me a bed in the next room. He would inform the authorities. With that he went back to bed.

I was dismayed. How long would I have to wait here until they got about to 'informing the authorities?' I could just see it happening: getting stuck in the cogwheels of the impossible bureaucracy. Would it be another week here before I got home? The stubborn impassiveness of many officials had taught me to try to avoid dealing with them except at the highest levels, where they had actual authority to make decisions and were often very gracious and anxious to help a foreign *mehman*, guest. So much for my feelings on equality. Or was it two different things, dealing with a person and dealing with a representative of authority? There definitely was a difference. I could accept a *babu*, or lowly clerk as an equal and a friend, but it was just impractical to try to deal with him in matters where a higher authority was involved.

Someone, it must have been the policeman who had brought me, led me into a room where the lights were on and the ceiling *pankha*, fan, was going full blast, making the curtains flutter and filling the room with the noise of an approaching helicopter. There was a small wooden sign-board over the door with the letters AHO in white paint. There was no-one inside, I had the room to myself.

The next thing I remember is waking up. A dozen or so sepoys were at various stages of having breakfast, dressing into uniform or washing themselves and shaving under the spicket in the courtyard. I was thirsty. Getting up, I walked out into the courtyard to the water tap that was open and flowing full force. This happened whenever there was water in the pipes, usually for an hour a day. I had used to think it a terrible waste of a valuable resource, but it really wasn't so stupid after all, if you thought about it. No-one could leave the tap on all day, which would cause far greater waste, and with a constant flow in a given area for an hour on end, the open sewers got at least enough flow to dispose of most of the sewage that had gathered in them. If the Municipal Corporation or the Cantonment board allocated water to the different areas of town in the right sequence, the whole sewage system would get flushed out every day.

I drank and put my head under the steady stream. To my surprise, I wasn't stiff. I hadn't slept for more than a couple of hours. Maybe there had been no time to get stiff. Or the heat had helped to keep me supple. I hardly recognized the fellow who had brought me in when he appeared before me in his civvies[5] with a towel in his hand, asking how I had slept while he waited for his turn under the tap.

I asked if I could ring my home now and speak with my wife, tell her I was all right and would be back soon. He took me over to the table where the night watch had been sitting and asked one of the three sitting at breakfast there to dial for me. A police officer walked up to the desk and told me in English that he had informed the authorities and that they would take me into town for debriefing right away. I would be home by nine o'clock. That was a good time, I thought, if my family was at home, not too early. Little Anna would be awake by then too. I had started telling the clerk the number to dial before the officer interrupted, now switching between Urdu and English numbers as is common usage, the policeman dialling got utterly confused and handed the telephone for me to dial. 7 − 6 − 5 − 5 − 3. I dialled and waited for the ring. Instead I got an engaged tone. It couldn't be, it wasn't seven-thirty in the morning yet. Who could be calling at this time of day? Had Anna lifted the receiver off the hook last night? She was always trying to reach the phone and play with it. It would hardly have been off the hook all night. Was it crossed lines? Often the line was 'busy' even though it was not actually in use. Sometimes one couldn't even get a dialling tone.

'Nashtah karo!' The sepoys at the table invited me to join them in their breakfast of hot, sweet, buffalo-milk tea and freshly baked *naan* bread. Someone rinsed out a cup with a little tea from the pot and

[5]Pakistanis wear normal shilwar-kameez suits as nightclothes, in fact the word 'pyjama' refers to a tighter cut of the same outfit preferred by Hindus in India.

Freedom

filled it up for me. Another tore his bread in half and gave me a piece. I was in so much turmoil over not being able to make contact with my family that I didn't have an appetite. I chewed on a few bits of bread and said that I would like to try calling again.

Saturday, 7.30 a.m.

This time I heard it ring, but before the first ring had ended the phone was off the hook and someone was saying 'hello'. It wasn't Marja-Liisa's voice. Why wasn't she at the phone? Why was someone else attending our line? Had Marja-Liisa left? The churning in my stomach turned into a shrinking feeling until I realized it was Maija-Leena's, our mission's field representative's reassuring voice.

'Is Marja-Liisa there?' I asked straight away, incapable of making any small talk, afraid that she might have been sent away with the children. I had to know.

'Yes, she's here . . .'

'Is she is up yet, can I talk with her, Maija, or will it wake up the kids if you go into the bedroom to get her?'

'She is up already. She just spoke to the Deputy Superintendent of Police on the phone a minute ago. Here she is . . .'

'Marja-Liisa? I'm free, I'm coming home . . .' I couldn't finish the sentence for emotion.

'Are you OK, I mean well?' she asked.

'Yes, I'm fine.'

'Really? Are you really OK?' She sought reassurance.

'Yes, really!' For the first time the tears came, there no longer being any need for defence mechanisms to be in place. 'We'll be together again soon!'

'You don't need to say anything,' Marja-Liisa comforted me as I hung wordless and tearful on the line. 'The police just told me they found you and that they would bring you in.'

'OK,' I managed, and gently laid the receiver in its cradle, not wanting to hang up, but not able to continue either.

Escape from terror

'Tears of joy,' I explained to the policemen sitting around me, as I wiped my cheeks on my sleeve.

They nodded their approval with big smiles. Simple men who understood such simple and straightforward emotion.

'Ek cup aur pio,' the one who was already pouring me a second cup of tea instructed. I was glad for the diversion, to be able to concentrate on the hot, sweet brew as the men at the table studied my face with an open curiosity and others milled around as Pakistanis tend to do when something out of the ordinary is happening.

'This man will take you in to the Gharbi Thana where the DSP is waiting to see you . . .'

I looked up from my cup of tea to see that the officer in charge of the police station had come up and was addressing me. A junior constable was beside him, smiling that he was going to do the honours. I rose and left to a chorus of 'Khuda hafiz,' 'God be your protector.' He led me out of the half-height door, like those that have been used in fortifications for as long as men have built them, so that an intruder would have to bend over while coming in, rendering himself defenceless to those waiting on the inside.

It felt uncanny to be entering the real world again, the world of normality, where I could move about freely and not be haunted by that hunted feeling. It was only now that I began to feel that it was over. By light of day and with traffic coming and going the surroundings seemed natural once again. Perhaps it was my escort telling me that he would be taking me in to the West Cantonment Police Headquarters by car, and in almost the same breath saying there was no police vehicle available, which brought me back. The wonderful, exhilarating, and – only sometimes to the point of distraction frustrating – orchestrated mess of Pakistani life hit me with full force.

We stood there at the side of the early morning road, the two of us like schoolboys waiting for the bus. A red Datsun pickup with a wooden cage extending the size of its floor approached slowly, picking up and dropping off people as it went. A conductor perched on the top shoved people together more tightly to make room for the newcomers and banged on the roof of the cab to indicate when the driver should start or stop. My escort stepped out into the road with his arm out to indicate that the driver should stop. Before the pickup had come to a full stop the driver, a middle-aged Afghan with fair complexion and patriarchal beard, began fiddling in his wallet for his papers or money, or both, protesting that he was innocent, just a poor driver. The policeman cut him off and told him to empty the truck, he was commandeering it. The driver was at once at ease again: if that's all it was . . . it could be talked about; it would mean he was owed a favour from this cop in the future. His half-hearted, good-natured protest led to a reasonable compromise: only the three people seated next to him in the cab would have to get out and onto the back, and the driver could let the people get off where they had planned, so he wouldn't have to refund any money to aggravated passengers. In all it was a reasonable deal, a compromise such as life is made of in the subcontinent. We drove alongside the canal for several kilometres, stopping every few hundred metres to let someone off where I, for one, could see no reason to disembark. Still I had no exact idea of where we were until we reached the intersection with Khyber Road at the 'Spin Juma'at', the White Mosque of University Town next to the Khyber Hospital. It was the first landmark I recognized, I was home again, a fish back in the water, a bird out of its cage. I wondered that in four years of living in Peshawar I had never had cause to turn right at the Spin Juma'at, except that time I had been looking for the Christian colony at the University Forestry Institute and had taken a wrong turn, but noticed right away and not continued along the road we had just come in on.

Here on Khyber Road, or Jamrud Road, depending on who was talking, life went on as usual. Nothing had changed. Had I changed? Some things I saw with new eyes, as if for the first time, mainly people. How many of the people doing business in the unending bazaar strung out along the road were involved in trying to raise ransom money for a kidnapped relative? How many accepted kidnapping as a way of life in these parts?

We passed the spot where I had once noticed the Chief Minister of

the North West Frontier Province inspecting a construction site. I had
stopped the car hoping to get a short interview. The police and
security men had tried to ward me off, but the Chief Minister had
waved to them to let me through. I had told him about our difficulties
getting building permits for church schools. He promised to help, and
probably did, because we eventually got the building permit. The
project was well under way, and Christian children would soon be
able to move into the new classrooms where they would have proper
desks and trained teachers. It was one of the most far-reaching projects
we had as a mission within the local church. Children's, even the
whole church's future could be changed. Children received Christian
education, and we were determined on having teachers who cared
about them, qualified and willing to give them a new outlook on life,
maybe even a new lease on life. The minority Christian community
faced immense difficulties in their future. Increasingly more Christian
farmers were leaving their unviable plots in the Punjab or their
untenable positions as share-croppers and were coming to the cities in
search of work. For the most part, the only job they could get was a
sweepers. But even that was changing. With more and more Muslim
jobless some were finding themselves forced into the demeaning work
of the casteless untouchables, so even this otherwise despised
occupation was no longer exclusively reserved for the religious
minorities. What would Christians do when they couldn't get work
as sweepers anymore? Schooling was imperative but for Christians and
Hindus it was not easy to get. The plot of land our mission had
procured to build a school here in University Town lay behind us. We
had never been able to build on it. Agitators had incited students to
vandalize the building site whenever labourers showed up. Even our
lawyer's motorbike's tyres had been slashed when he tried to negotiate
a solution. No-one really wanted segregated Christian schools for our
community's children, but there seemed no other viable way. Even
the older well-educated Christians who had been to government
schools with the majority community in British days and soon after
independence and had been able to make friends with Muslims, who
were now in influential positions, had to admit that sweepers' children

Freedom

didn't get the same, even-handed treatment they had received back in those days when tolerance and equality had been virtues.

The driver was still chatting to my escort when we turned onto Sir Syed Road, where the school and cathedral church were. The last of the passengers had got off back in University Town. As we drove past St John's Cathedral School for Christian children with its 500 pupils and the Cathedral church, I wondered how only a week could have passed since I had been on my way here for the bishop's consecration. They had had to manage without me this week, they should realize now that they could do without me in my managerial role in future as well. Then I could concentrate on working more with the church's most important resource, the people. I wanted now more than ever to be able to motivate and equip individuals for service in the church. People who would not back away from challenges, not give up in the face of adversity, be willing to make sacrifices for Christ's sake.

Opposite the school, the Cultural Centre of the Islamic Republic of Iran shone white in the bright morning light. The bomb that had gone off there a couple of years earlier had fortunately detonated on a Sunday, when none of the children were at school to be injured by the flying glass from all the windows on the side facing the centre. The bomb had been meant for the offices of the *Frontier Post*, then a new newspaper still enthusiastic about reporting things as it saw them. It had been a bad year for bombs in our area. Within a 300-metre radius of our house there had been terrorist bombings at the PIA building, British Airways, the *Frontier Post*, the hockey stadium and the United States Consulate. Everybody had told us: 'The Cantonment is the safest place to live, just don't let your children out onto the street or they will be gone!' Well, it had been safe enough considering the circumstances in Peshawar, our home had only been broken into once, and then only the mission's video camera was stolen.

As we pulled into the dusty drive of the West Cantonment Police HQ, two policemen issued from an open doorway and directed me into the DSP's office with the information that he would be arriving shortly. For once it wasn't just said as a consolation. He actually did arrive within ten minutes, and when he did, the second-in-rank got up out of the DSP's seat he had been occupying behind the glass-topped desk well in time before his boss entered the room. My picture was under the glass. Now where had they got my passport photo?

Saturday, 8.30 a.m.

There must have been a crowd of sycophants waiting because hardly had he shaken my hand and congratulated me when the doorway blackened with people anxious to see him, to congratulate him 'on securing my release', 'on recovering the *angrez*'. He accepted the compliments graciously as I looked on. When the well-wishers, people who wanted to be remembered and members of the press who were grateful for information had been shooed out, he turned his attention to me. He lifted the glass top on his desk and drew out the passport photo. They had recovered it from the body of one of the thugs who had been shot. It must have been in my wallet.

'They want to put it in the paper,' he said 'together with the news about your release.'

I said I wanted as little noise made as possible, there was no need for the picture. Besides, who knew where the rest of the gang were, what if they wanted revenge for their two dead friends?

'There's no need for modesty,' he said, 'you are already famous! Everybody knows about you, you've been in the papers every day, you're a hero!'

He meant it well, but it was almost like a slap in the face, like being made fun of. If they knew what it had been like. And now to have to face the publicity . . .

'I don't want my picture in the paper,' I said, determined to stop him from giving it to the press. 'I don't want the gang seeing my picture, for security reasons,' I added, giving him grounds he could appreciate as a law enforcer if he weren't able to understand my need for privacy.

We went through the case, I was debriefed. He had one important thing to say before anything else was said: the police had been working day and night, there had been terrible pressure on them from the political authorities and embassies to produce, but this had never happened before, that a foreigner was released without ransom and returned alive on his own.

'Your release without ransom and your coming back on foot all alone from Tribal Territory it is a miracle of God!' he said, in a rare moment of humble recognition that the police had not been able to achieve anything. It endeared him to me. Such straightforwardness was truly out of the ordinary.

He told me that he himself had gone in plain clothes into the tribal area to try to pick up a lead, but they had not been able to make any contacts. When he heard that I had come through Nasir Bagh Camp number two, he shook his head in disbelief:

'We were in that camp last night negotiating with tribal elders just before you walked through, trying to get them to locate you for us, and you were already free, walking towards the meeting! It really is a miracle!' he exclaimed.

He drew out a newspaper clipping showing the dead bodies of the two who had been shot, asking if I recognized them. They were definitely the two ringleaders, the one who interrogated me and had taken charge of me once they had got me into the car and the one with the bushy beard who had led the attack on my car, smashing in the window and then trying to start my car. I shuddered to look at it. They were dead. Everybody knew it. It was right there in the paper for everyone to see.

'How did it happen?' I asked.

He drew yet another clipping out of a folder and showed it to me, a group of fifteen to twenty tribesmen gathered in class-photo formation with their weapons.

'These men shot them, they call themselves the "Islami lashkar", the "Islamic host". They wanted to get rid of these bad elements, had been looking out for them for some six months, but this one, the one with the beard who goes by the alias "Sher Ali", "Ali's Lion", is also known as the "Phantom". He hadn't been sighted once in the last six months. They were heading through Barra for Tirah in a rented

Datsun pickup when one of the "lashkar" recognized him and ordered them to stop at their road-block. They made a break for it, there was a shoot-out, two of them died on the spot and a third was wounded, but managed to escape . . .'

He watched me closely to see if I believed him. Why? Wasn't it the truth, the whole truth and nothing but the truth? Or was it a smoke-screen intended to blind the public's eyes to what really had happened? My guard had claimed they had been shot in cold blood, not in a shoot-out, not trying to escape. Was the truth somewhere in-between? Were the police or the para-police, the khasadaars, the ones who had done the shooting, but needed to have it look as if they were not involved so there would be no reprisals against the police from related tribals? The police had to be careful . . . He had one argument to lend credence to his version:

'The Islamics found this passport photo of you on the body of one of the dead criminals along with a cheque for one lac rupees in your name. They gave us the photo, that's how we came to know, but they wanted to keep the cheque . . .'

I would have to block that cheque, fast! What if they managed to cash it?!

The DSP wanted to know where I had been held. He couldn't work out how I had walked all the way past Nasir Bagh without running into a single road-block.

'I didn't come by road, I crossed the desert in a straight line.'

'But we had Barra hermetically sealed, under siege, you would have had to pass our men somewhere!'

'I wasn't anywhere near Barra, I came straight from the mountains north of Jamrud, a two hour walk from there. And I circled Jamrud too, never entering the town. The place where I was held was supposed to be Orakzai territory, the man kept calling it "Ajjilabad".'

The DSP turned to a lesser officer whose Pushto was obviously better than his. Neither of them could think of a place called Ajjilabad. Then the subordinate broke into a smile:

'Of course, "*ajjil*-abad", Pushto for "Dwelling of Death!" He just wanted to scare you, he made up the name. "Ajjil" is a rare word!'

Freedom

I explained exactly how to get there, but added that the man who held me wasn't really the one at fault. The police didn't even make any notes. I guessed that we all agreed that my guard should be left alone, after all, he had freed me.

Humphrey Peters and Ron Pont, two close friends, came into the office with the intention of taking me home. We embraced. It was pure release to be with valued friends again. The DSP called the debriefing off, but insisted we all have a cup of tea before they took me home, saying that he had been planning to take me home personally in his own car, but understood that I would want to be accompanied by my Pakistani and English friends.

Sunday, 10.30 a.m.

The ride along Mall Road was short. Turning at the Telephone and Telegraph office, passing Edwardes College on the one side and the saint's tomb on the other, symbols of the Christian and Islamic worlds lived in, we arrived at the gate opening onto the cluster of four homes where we rented a house. The gate-keeper heard the car coming and was already undoing the latch when the driver sounded the horn. Someone inside the house heard the car pull up the drive and was opening the massive, almost square, palisander-wood door to our living room that was always sticking because of the strain on the hinges, no matter how tight I did the hinges or how much I planed off the edges . . .

The ordeal was over. Marja-Liisa stood with Anna in her arms and Tuomas and Henrik at her side. Behind them were more people than I could take in. My family filled my eyes, to see them once again . . . To be able to embrace my family again was something so tender I had never experienced it before. A new beginning.

The others, our Pakistani and missionary friends who had melted away for that first, unique moment came back to embrace us as a family. People were asking what they could get me, what I would like to eat or drink.

'I need a bath, just a bath . . .'

My family sat around the bathtub and listened as I related what had happened, although Anna at two would have rather joined me in the water. How was she to understand that the water was too dirty for her to play in? The boys counted the open blisters on my feet and came up with an even dozen, Marja-Liisa asked about the scab on my right shoulder blade. That was what had hurt most those first few days. A look in the mirror revealed that it had the shape of a rifle muzzle, a perfect circle. It was strange that I couldn't recall when that wound had been inflicted. None of the blows had seemed particularly hard, I only remembered that the little man with the pock-marked face had hit me on the head and shoulders with his automatic's butt. How had I come out unscathed?

I heard the other side of the story, the pain and uncertainty my family and friends had been through from beginning to end, the conflicting reports they had received and the comfort they had been given by our local friends, Muslim, Christian and Hindu. I must have spent an hour in the tub. When I got out of the water when we had been through the major details of the past week, Marja-Liisa commented on my having lost weight. I climbed on the scales, tipping them at 74 kilograms. I had lost seven kg in as many days and was even a little below my ideal weight. We laughed about bread twice a day being an ideal weight-watcher's diet.

I was still drying myself off when the first of what seemed an endless number of phone calls came through. My release had been communicated around the world already, just as the media had carried my kidnapping immediately and broken the news in Canada and Germany the same day, in Finland the next. I couldn't fathom it, how the media had reported on my kidnapping when I myself hadn't known the whole time whether even my family knew what had happened. Phone calls came in from Canada, Germany, California, Finland. I was overwhelmed and felt so small in the light of God's great mercy. It truly was a miracle!

EPILOGUE

Today is 15 September 1993. It has taken me three years to the day to recount the events presented in this book. One of my close friends and colleagues originally counselled me to 'write the story quickly, before I began to embellish and exaggerate it'. It was good advice and well meant. It motivated me to sketch out the basic course of events in the first week or two after my release. On the other hand, there was a lot of material that I was not yet ready to deal with. Despite admonitions from friends and acquaintances in Pakistan, including the Governor of the North West Frontier Province and the half-brother of the Chief Minister to make a book out of the events, there were months on end when I had to leave the project untouched. At times the whole idea of a book was repulsive to me. There were times when I simply didn't have the time or the strength to work on it. About a year ago, independent of increasing pressure from others to finish the book, I began to feel the urge to 'close the chapter' myself.

Going over the material, I realized that my exercise in writing had been in reality a therapeutic effort. Having finished the basic story, I found that the events no longer haunted me on a daily basis as they had while the story had remained untold. With the more than two years distance from the events I also became aware of how I had written the whole story only for myself. With time I became able, in a sense, to look at the story from the outside. It gained some of the bird's-eye perspective necessary for telling to someone who was not there. Re-reading it, I recognized how little any other reader would be able to comprehend without substantial enlargement on the basics of every-day life in Pakistan. I hope that the result is a book more about Pakistan than about a week in September 1990. This view helped me to overcome many of the inhibitions I had about publishing the story at all. Another help in this regard were the comments of friends who knew more of the details of the story and how I had experienced them. They seemed sincere in asking me to share these with a large public that had a genuine and honest interest in knowing the actual course of events and was no longer driven by sensationalist appetites. Particularly how I had felt the proximity of God in those days seemed to be a matter of keen interest. If my account helps anyone to recognize how close God is to them in their time of need, the book will have served a purpose.

People often ask questions such as: 'How much did the police (and your family) know about what had happened to you?' 'Who were the kidnappers and why did they pick you?' 'How did they catch and kill the two criminals?' 'Why did the man finally let you go?' While there are still no clear-cut answers to some of these questions after three years, some elements were established quite soon afterwards with a reasonable degree of certainty.

My family found out almost immediately that I had been abducted, even though no demand for ransom was ever conveyed and the kidnappers themselves did not telephone as they had promised. There had, in fact, been two eye-witnesses of the actual kidnapping. One was a *tonga-wallah*, a horse-and-cart taxi driver, who was within clear vision and hearing range, but managed to stay out of the way. The other was a shopkeeper in the bazaar we had just left when the gang took me. Both gave testimony to the police, albeit confusing and, in part, contradictory. They had stated that the men while attacking my car had been shouting Islamic slogans. I certainly didn't hear anything so refined from their mouths, but then maybe they changed their tune once the window was bashed in. It is possible that they did shout 'Allah-hu-akbar' (God is greater) right at the outset to ensure that no-one interfered, thinking theirs a just cause. My experience of the men was that they were only nominal Muslims and criminal elements, not fundamentalist Islamics.

The police were also looking for a blue getaway car the whole time. When they heard from me that it had been green they were perplexed

Epilogue

wondered if my colour-blindness was at fault. But I never confused blue and green, only red and green tones. That score was settled when a junior officer who was a native Pushto speaker asked what the eye-witnesses had said in that language, then laughed when he heard it: *shin*, in Pushto, means blue and green. The colours are not differentiated per se. If one meant blue as opposed to green, he would say *'aasmaani shin'* the *shin* of the sky.

One of the witnesses told the police that there had only been three men. That caused a problem when the two ringleaders were shot and one of their accomplices, also 'positively identified' at the time they were shot, was wounded but escaped anyway. Who was left to guard me? Had they managed to sell me off to someone else like Joseph to the Midianites? How would they track me down? What was worse, who would claim credit and assume responsibility for the killings?

While the Station Chief of the Barra Gate precinct bragged to me that he 'had personally shot the culprits', the DIG police assured me that the police had not been involved in the apprehension or shooting at all. He had presented a newspaper clipping showing a group of some twenty tribesmen standing with their rifles for a group photo. They called themselves 'Islami Lashkar', the host of Islam, a self-styled law-and-order enforcement agency in the tribal territories. I was told that they had kept the cheque for 100,000 rupees I had been carrying, in hopes of being able to cash it as their reward. Maija-Leena had had the foresight to have the bank draft blocked on the very first day and so it was worthless. I had the funny feeling that the 'Lashkar' version was just a smoke-screen. The authorities couldn't afford to be implicated. Any way you looked at it, it was bad public relations. If they had killed the men, then they had needlessly endangered my life by doing so. Furthermore, it would have only served as an invitation for reprisals from the tribals against officials and institutions of the government.

The police already had some relatives of the gang members in custody before my kidnapping, and one of the demands of the group was the release of those prisoners in exchange for me. If the story was true that the men had been shot in cold blood at point-blank range in a summary execution, then no-one would want to take the 'credit.'

Escape from terror

A few days after my release I was taken to see the Political Agent for the tribal agency I had been held in. The Political Agent offered chicken sandwiches, tea and confessions. His troops, para-military para-police 'khasadaars' (special forces) had been somehow involved. The police had no access to the tribal area and had not been involved. He stopped short of an outright admission and couched his confession with the handy option of a religious, and therefore untouchable group being involved as well. It was he who told me that they had hermetically sealed Barra, believing me to be held there (I was in Jamrud district), and had met with tribal representatives of the Afridi tribe in the very refugee camp I had walked through the very night I did so, trying to get them to locate and release me themselves. There had been talk of the army coming in and bulldozing some villages again, if they weren't forthcoming. He also told me that the Tribal Elders thought I had put a curse on the gang, and that was why the two had been shot. No-one knew at that meeting that they were all barking up the wrong tree: my guard told me he was an Orakzai, a completely different tribe. If that was so, it meant I was no longer in Afridi territory or under the jurisdiction of an Afridi *jirga*. Perhaps that was why they couldn't find me. The plan to take me to Tirah, the heart of Orakzai territory, fitted in best with my guard's explanation and the inability of the gang to pass me off in Barra or Jamrud.

The Pakistani government, lobbied heavily by the Finnish and Canadian Embassies, exerted tremendous pressure on the tribal leaders to find and release me. The highest officers in the provincial police took a personal interest and made great personal efforts to locate me, to a large extent, as one of them told me, because the government was putting pressure on them to produce. Canadian, Finnish and even CIA representatives had closely monitored the incident. The CIA had been reportedly very helpful, putting its own personnel in the field on the case.

Kimmo and Eija Pulkkinen of the Finnish Embassy in Islamabad were particularly concerned and helpful. Knowing that I needed a break and a short time away from all the visitors and telephone calls, they invited us to stay with them for a few days. The embassy staff

Epilogue

debriefed me and I was taken to see the Inspector General of Police and the Provincial Governor, who also wanted to get to the bottom of things.

One of the strangest things was the jealousy that some people felt. Someone in the church was angry that I had 'spoiled' the consecration by disappearing that day. Hundreds of guests at the function had not even eaten. The sixty chickens that had been cooked were not touched. The afternoon celebration had turned into a prayer meeting. One of the church leaders commented afterwards 'Ap ko barri izzat milgai hai', 'You have received great esteem!'

Whereas the reader will find a trove of emotional material in this account and be able to analyse the psyche of this hostage, I have not related anything of the post-trauma effects on me and my family. That could be a whole story of its own.

Some of the more immediate effects were a need for acceptance, warmth and understanding. The fact that most people were intrigued by my experience became a burden. I was happy to share my experiences with those whom I knew cared for me personally, but was put off by those who just wanted to hear an exciting story. Worst were those who wanted to make capital out of my experience. I was baffled that many people couldn't relate to me in that situation. Perhaps the worst was the sense of helplessness I had at having re-won the family and friends I had already inwardly said goodbye to, but not being able to do anything in a significantly different way. Not being able to make anything new out of the gift of a new life.

To put it in one sentence, I wanted to be accepted for who and what I am, not for what I'd been through.

GLOSSARY

Aadmi (Urdu) man, person

Afghans the residents of Afghanistan belong to many different peoples, the majority of those living in the eastern half of the country are Pathans (see below)

Afridi one of the larger Pathan tribes living near Peshawar

Ahl (Arabic) a people in a particular position as opposed to 'qoum'; cf. hebrew 'ha'aam'

Ahl-e-dhimma (Arabic) a 'protected', i.e. subjected people with certain rights and liberties including limited religious autonomy

Al-Masih (Arabic) the Messiah, Christ

Algebra (from the Arabic) the power(ful way)

Ali (n.p.) one of the first califs, a 'patron saint' particularly of shi'a Muslims

Angrez (subcontinent) corruption of 'anglais', perhaps via the Portugese of Goa

Assalamo-aleikum (Arabic, common Islamic) his peace be upon you; cf. Hebrew 'shalom aleihem'

Asuul (from Arabic, Urdu) principle

Ba-ilqul (Arabic, Urdu) completely, by all means

Babu (Urdu) the lowest rank of office clerk

Badmaash (Urdu) hooligan

Baittho (Urdu) imp. pl. sit!

Bakshish (common) gift, alms, reward etc.

Bazaar (common) a (permanent) line of shop–booths

Bharay-huay (Urdu) filled, loaded

Burqa (Urdu, Pushto) a woman's veil, originating in the subcontinent, completely covering the body from head to foot like a tent; the

Glossary

original burqa used by Hindu women was open in the front from the waist down so the hands could be used

Chadar (Urdu, Pushto from Persian) a sheet used as a wrap-around cover for many purposes, by women who do not use the burqa as a means of maintaining purdah

Chai (common) tea

Chann (Punjabi) the ritual shaving of a baby's first hair

Chapatti (Urdu, Punjabi) a thin pancake of unleavened bread eaten with curries

Charpai (common) a 'four-legger', meaning a string bed on a frame

Chowk (common) a crossing, square or 'piazza'

Chup (Urdu) imp. sg. silent!

Daksun (Pushto, corrupted) pickup truck used as rural taxi; from 'Datsun'

Daksunwalla (Pushto, corrupted) driver of above

Dal, daal (common) lentil, gram

Dalaal (Urdu) broker, 'fence', middleman

Danda (Urdu) club, stick used as weapon or implement of punishment

Dari old Persian dialect spoken as the lingua franca of Afghanistan

Dawa (coll. Pushto) either for du'a (see below) or daawa(t) – proselytization

Dijiye (Urdu) polite for 'give'

Du'a (Arabic, common) voluntary prayer

Dukan (common) small shop or booth in bazaar

Eid (common, via Arabic from Latin) two major Islamic religious festivals; cf. 'the ides of March'

Ek cup aur pio (Urdu) drink another cup!

Farangi (subcontinent) European; from 'Frank'

Farsi modern Persian as spoken in Iran and parts of Central Asia

Fateha (Arabic) a Surah of the Qur'an spoken as a prayer during namaaz and in memory of the deceased

Fouwara (common) fountain

Gali (Hindko, Pahari) a village on the mountain

Gornament (common, corruption from English) government

Haafiz (Persian) protector

Hadd (Urdu) beat it! back off! get out of the way!

Hadith (Arabic) collection of recognized authoritative interpretations of Islamic theology based on Qur'an, Sunnat and the life of Muhammad

Hava (Urdu, from Persian) air, wind, breeze

Hotel, hotl (common) a wayside stall where tea and aliments are served, in some cases beds are available

Hujra (Pushto) men's house used communally by villagers

Illaqa (Urdu) area, locale

Isa' (n.p. via Arabic) Jesus

Isai (common) a Christian, a sweeper

Izzat (common) honour, renown, good reputation

Jamaa'at (Urdu) class, party

Ji han (Urdu) yes (sir)!

Jirga (Pushto) council of elders

Jor (Pushto) healthy, well

Juma'at (Pushto) mosque

Juma' (Arabic) Friday (main time of prayer with sermon)

Kaghazat (Urdu) papers, identification

Kal (Urdu) tomorrow

Kali thorri (common) a cucumber-like squash

Kalma (Arabic) the basic creed of Islam: 'there is no God besides God and Muhammed is his apostle'

Kana (Pushto) injective 'why don't you', 'won't you'

Kayna (Pushto) sit

Kha (Pushto) yes

Khasadaar (Pushto) law enforcement officer of the Political Agent

Khatarnak (common) dangerous, hazardous

Khuda (Persian) God

Koi bat nahin (Urdu) it doesn't matter

Kor (Pushto) fortified dwelling or group of dwellings

Lal (subcontinent) ruby

Layn-dayn (Urdu) give and take; system of reciprocity

Lota (common) teapot shaped water container used in toilet

Machhar (Urdu) mosquito

Glossary

Maghrib (Arabic) West, evening prayer

Maiday (Pushto) bread

Majboori (Urdu, common) necessity, compulsion, duress

Malik (Pushto) local chieftain or landlord (*urdu*, *maalik*, landlord, owner)

Mall Road main (parade, promenade) thoroughfare in the British cantonment

Mantra (Sanskrit) secret holy syllable or 'word' used in yoga meditation

Margiya (Urdu) died

Marmar (common) marble

Mehman (common) guest

Mithrab (Arabic) arch denoting the qibla

Muezzin (Arabic) one who performs the call to prayer (azaan)

Murree (n.p.) resort city in the mountains north of Islamabad

Naan (Urdu) leavened flatbread

Naashtah (Urdu) breakfast

Namaaz (common) Islamic ritual prayer

Nashah (common) narcotic, drug inducing hallucination or well-being

Naswaar (common) snuff-like tobacco powder kept in the cheek or under the tongue

Orakzai (n.p.) tribe of Pathans

Pak (common) pure, holy

Pani to dena (Urdu) give me (a drink of) water!

Pankha (Urdu) fan, originally a large sheet suspended from the rafters of a high ceiling and propelled by a servant pulling a rope with his toes from the outside verandah

Pathans a people of aryan descent living both sides of the Pakistan-Afghanistan border comprising twenty to thirty millions

Pikhawar northern Pushto for Peshawar

Pukka (Urdu) permanent, solid, well-built, sure

Punjabi inhabitants of the Punjab, the language of the Punjab

Purdah (common) seclusion of women, 'veil', curtain

Pushto language of the Pathans, also pronounced 'Pukhtoo'

Qazi (Arabic) Islamic (hereditary) judge

Qibla (Arabic) the direction of Mecca

Qur'an the holy book of Islam, 'repetition'

Ravi (n.p.) one of the five major rivers of the Punjab

Resham (Urdu, common) silk

Riksha (subcontinent, Southeast Asia) small cart, vehicle or bicycle used as taxi

Roshndaan (Urdu, from Persian) 'giver of light'; ventilator high in the wall

Roti (Urdu) bread, food

Roti to hai (Urdu) there must be something to eat

Saddar (Urdu) main, chief, president

Salaat (Arabic) theological term for Islamic ritual prayer

Sang (Urdu) stone

Sayviyyan (Urdu) spaghetti-like sweet dish

Seb (Pushto, coll.) Sahib

Shahadat (Arabic) confession of faith, creed

Shamiana (Urdu) tent, awning set up for festivities

Shariah (Arabic) Islamic canonical law

Shariat same as above

Sher (common) lion, tiger

Shifaarish (Urdu) intercession on someone's behalf by a person with connections

Shilwar-kameez (Urdu) national dress of Pakistani Muslims

Shin (Pushto) green, blue

Shirk (Arabic) the principal heresy against Islam, i.e. that God is associated with another being outside his own

Sohan (Punjabi) golden

Spin (Pushto) white

Sunnat (Arabic) canonical Islamic tradition

Surah (Arabic) a chapter of the Qur'an

Takra (Pushto) strong, healthy

Tarkari (Pushto) curry

Taurat (from Arabic) the Torah, in Islamic usage the Old Testament (except for the Psalms)

Tikala (Pushto) bread

Tonga (common) horse-drawn two-wheeled carriage

Glossary

U-aleikum-assalam (Arabic, common) and peace also be with you

Uska (Pushto) drink

Uttho (Urdu) get up!

Wadi a canyon-like seasonal river-bed

Wagon (common) a van-type minibus

Wallah (Urdu) postposition denoting one who does or is something relating to the preceding word

Worka (Pushto) bring! give!

Wuzu (Arabic) ritual Islamic washings preceding salaat

Zaalim (Urdu) a cruel, unjust person

Zenith (from Arabic) the highest point a heavenly body reaches in the sky

Zindabad (Urdu) long live! viva!